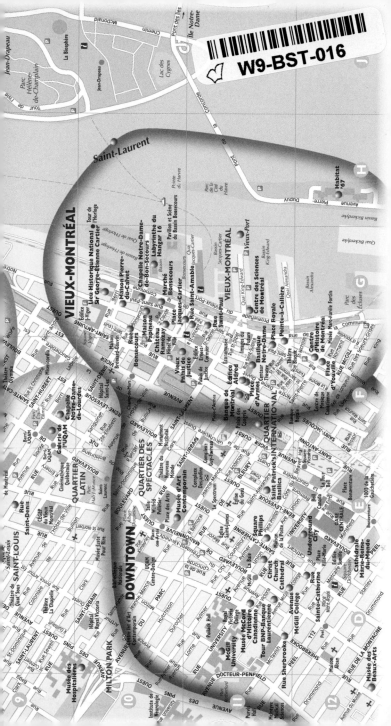

MONTRÉAL

How to Use This Book

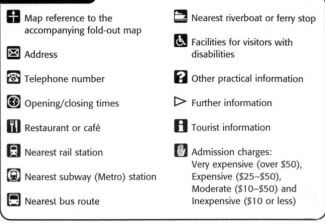

KEY TO SYMBOLS

✚ Map reference to the accompanying fold-out map

✉ Address

☎ Telephone number

🕐 Opening/closing times

🍴 Restaurant or café

🚆 Nearest rail station

Ⓜ Nearest subway (Metro) station

🚌 Nearest bus route

🛳 Nearest riverboat or ferry stop

♿ Facilities for visitors with disabilities

❓ Other practical information

▷ Further information

ℹ Tourist information

✋ Admission charges:
Very expensive (over $50),
Expensive ($25–$50),
Moderate ($10–$50) and
Inexpensive ($10 or less)

This guide is divided into four sections

• Essential Montréal: An introduction to the city and tips on making the most of your stay.

• Montréal by Area: We've broken the city into five areas, and recommended the best sights, shops, entertainment venues, nightlife and restaurants in each one. Suggested walks help you to explore on foot.

• Where to Stay: The best hotels, whether you're looking for luxury, budget or something in between.

• Need to Know: The info you need to make your trip run smoothly, including getting about by public transportation, weather tips, emergency phone numbers and useful websites.

Navigation In the Montréal by Area chapter, we've given each area its own color, which is also used on the locator maps throughout the book and the map on the inside front cover.

Maps The fold-out map accompanying this book is a comprehensive street plan of Montréal. The grid on this fold-out map is the same as the grid on the locator maps within the book. We've given grid references within the book for each sight and listing.

Contents

Introducing Montréal

Montréal is one of the world's great cities, a stylish and laid-back metropolis with superb museums, excellent restaurants, first-rate shopping, a vibrant cultural life and a cosmopolitan population that works and plays with a broad smile on its face.

Nestled between the banks of the Saint Lawrence River and the slopes of Mont-Royal, the heart of the island city is a wonderful mixture of old and new: from the cobbled streets, historic squares and fine buildings of Vieux-Montréal, the city's earliest incarnation after the arrival of French settlers in 1642, to the busy modern streets of downtown, with its many skyscrapers and dazzling underground malls and walkways. Farther afield is the site of the 1976 Olympic Games, now an attraction in its own right.

Montréal, of course, owes much of its considerable charm—not least its superb food—to its French heritage, one that has made it the largest French-speaking city in the West after Paris. But to focus only on the city's French élan would be to miss the dynamic influence of its English-speaking residents and

a thriving immigrant population of 488,000, and the joie de vivre of a city that is young at heart.

True, there are problems—the winters can be cruel—but the old concerns of language, and of Montréal and the rest of Québec splitting from Canada, have receded. And Montréal is not just about food, fashion and entertainment, of style over substance. The fur trade and river traffic that made it rich may have declined, but this is still an economic powerhouse, still a place with a little grit to go with its wit.

So, a little piece of Europe in North America? Up to a point. French in taste? Definitely. English? In places, certainly. Canadian? That too. But also a dynamic, fun and fascinating city in its own right—whatever your language and whatever your fancy.

Facts + Figures

Population: 1,649,519 (2011 census).
Percentage of population that is French-speaking: 66.
Ranking: Canada's second-largest city after Toronto.
Area of city: 483sq km (188sq miles).
Islands making up city: 75.

PRINTED PAGE

Mordecai Richler brings the vibrant, hard-scrabble life of Montréal's Jewish community to life in the classic *St. Urban's Horseman* and *The Apprenticeship of Duddy Kravitz* (made into a film starring Richard Dreyfuss). Gabrielle Roy captured the struggles of the French-speaking population in *Bonheur d'Occasion* (translated as *The Tin Flute*).

BALCONVILLE

Many Montréalers live in duplexes and triplexes, stacked residences built in the 1930s and 1940s to house the city's blue-collar workers. Curving, wrought-iron staircases link the balconies of the various levels, a building strategy that saved interior space and inadvertently created pleasing places to gather round in the summer.

FAMOUS MONTRÉALERS

Montréal's famous include *Star Trek's* William Shatner, jazz great Oscar Peterson, novelist Mordecai Richler and poet-singer Leonard Cohen. Confederate president Jefferson Davis lived in the city after the American Civil War. Singer Céline Dion was born in Repentigny and film director Denys Arcand was born in Deschambeault.

... day in **place Jacques-Cartier** (▷ 37) in Vieux-Montréal. Walk southwest on rue Notre-Dame Ouest and visit the **Basilique Notre-Dame** (▷ 24–25). Spend the rest of the morning learning about the history of the city in the **Centre d'Histoire de Montréal** (▷ 26) or at nearby **Pointe-à-Callière** (▷ 30) and the **Musée d'Archéologie et d'Histoire de Montréal**.

Lunch Have a snack at **Olive et Gourmando** (▷ 44), a light meal in **L'Arrivage Café** (▷ 30) in the **Musée d'Archéologie**, or sample one of the many casual restaurants in the **Vieux-Port** area (▷ 32–33).

Afternoon If the weather is good, take a boat trip from one of the quays a few moments from the Musée d'Archéologie. Most last 60–90 minutes. If you are traveling with children you may want to visit the **Centre des Sciences de Montréal** (▷ 33–34) and other attractions on the waterfront piers. Then explore **rue Saint-Paul** (▷ 31) and the adjacent streets and squares, especially the **Chapelle Notre-Dame-de-Bon-Secours** (▷ 27) and **Château Ramezay** (▷ 34–35). The café in the latter makes a delightful place for afternoon tea. Also make time for shopping in the Marché Bonsecours (▷ 28).

Dinner Try **Toqué!** (▷ 44), one of Montréal's best restaurants for contemporary cuisine, but be sure to book well in advance. If you want to eat outdoors, reserve a terrace table at **Boris Bistro** (▷ 43).

Evening Take in a performance at the Centaur Theatre (▷ 42) or enjoy a drink with a waterfront view at **Pub St-Paul** (▷ 42). If the Cirque du Soleil (▷ 42, panel) is in town, try for last-minute tickets; otherwise check out what's on at **TOHU** circus arts center (▷ 105).

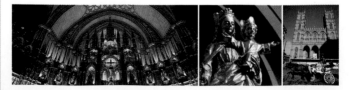

DAY 2

Morning Take a cab close to the Observatoire de l'Est in the **Parc du Mont-Royal** (▷ 72–73) for an overview of the city and a taste of the main park. Walk through the park to Avenue des Pins and then visit the **Musée McCord d'Histoire Canadienne** (▷ 55) and **Musée des Beaux-Arts** (▷ 54) or explore shops and malls such as La Baie and Centre Eaton above and below ground near rue Sainte-Catherine.

Lunch Downtown has many sandwich bars and inexpensive restaurants aimed at the area's working population. Or join the in-the-know locals for the outstanding Mediterranean fusion cuisine at the hip **Andiamo** restaurant (▷ 65).

Afternoon Either devote the afternoon to the many sights and shops of downtown or take the green Métro line to Pie-IX or Viau to see the sights on and around the **Parc Olympique** (▷ 90–91), especially the **Biodôme** (▷ 86–87) and **Jardin Botanique** (▷ 88–89).

Dinner You have innumerable choices for dinner, including options in the hip young Quartier Latin, one of the city's main areas for eating, drinking and nightlife. More sedate is boulevard Saint-Laurent above rue Sherbrooke, where you could try **Moishe's** (▷ 82), which has been serving sublime steaks since 1938, or **Schwartz's** (▷ 82) for their famous smoked meat.

Evening Head to the **Quartier Latin** (▷ 76) to enjoy its boisterous nightlife or, when in season, attend a ballet or a concert by Montréal's Orchestre Métropolitain. Also, during the summer, there will always be a festival of some sort taking place somewhere in the city. A good place to check is the place des Festivals, next to place des Arts.

These pages are a quick guide to the Top 25, which are described in more detail later. Here they are listed alphabetically and the tinted background shows the area they are in.

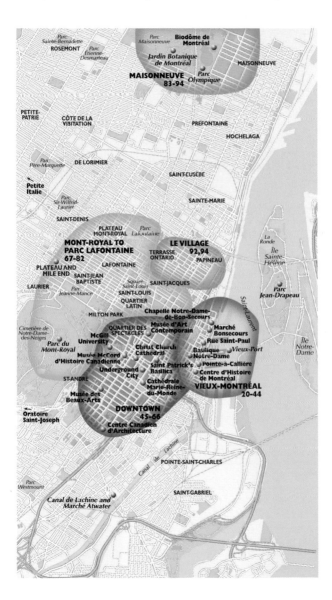

Shopping

Le shopping—now there's a word that crosses linguistic boundaries. Some Québécois may still *magasinent*, but the truly stylish *font le shopping*.

A Passion for Fashion
And Montréal is nothing if not stylish. The women dress well and, more tellingly, so do the men. Montréal is Canada's fashion capital, with a clothing industry that is the third-largest in North America. Several fashion schools churn out talent to keep the momentum brisk. And if you're looking for children's clothes, this is the place. Shoppers can find all the best stuff in the city's boutiques and department stores, but serious bargain-hunters head for the northern end of boulevard Saint-Laurent, to the dozens of clothing factories in the Chabanel area that sell to the public on Saturday mornings.

Outdoor Clothing
Trade in animal skins made the city wealthy in the first place, and given the climate, it's not surprising that furs are still popular winter wear. However, some designers have taken a different approach to cold-weather wear. The multilayer winter wear of Kanuk (▷ 79) is stylish and comfortable.

Antiques
Montréal's age makes it a tempting prospect for antiques collectors. Dozens of shops in Westmount, along the west end of rue

---

SMART SHOPPING

Don't even step into a store here without a copy of *Smart Shopping Montréal* in your pocket. Updated every year, this no-nonsense compendium is the guide to everything from haute couture to second-hand furs. Although the emphasis is on where to get the best buys (often at astonishingly low prices), the author has a keen eye for quality. Whether it's children's toys or the best Montréal bagels, this book will lead you to it. Buy it in local bookstores or order pre-trip from www.smartshoppingmontreal.com.

From antiques shops and stylish shopping areas to bustling street markets, you can shop till you drop

Notre-Dame between avenue Atwater and rue Guy, and in Le Village cater to just about every taste, with furniture from colonial Québec to 1950s retro. Keep an eye out for rare books, as well as Victorian paintings, religious articles and decorations, china and silverware.

Arts and Crafts

Québec's artistic traditions reach back to the days of New France, when the colony's Catholic bishops kept dozens of artists hard at work, decorating churches with mosaics, paintings, sculptures and stained glass. Dozens of galleries cater to more modern tastes, with work by leading local artists like Paul Fenniak, Betty Goodwin and Jean-Louis Émond. If your tastes lean more to the traditional, consider a startlingly realistic wood carving by a Québec folk artist or a graceful soapstone sculpture by one of Canada's Inuit carvers.

Malls

While trendy shopping areas such as rue Saint-Denis, rue Sherbrooke in downtown and boulevard Saint-Laurent take the retail plaudits, don't overlook the joys of shopping under one roof. Montréal makes a great place for pre-Christmas shopping, thanks to its Underground City, which provides protection from the elements. Malls include Cours Mont-Royal, Les Promenades Cathédrale, Le Centre Eaton, place Ville-Marie and Montréal Trust, all interconnected, near the intersection of McGill and Sainte-Catherine streets.

Le Centre Eaton (top); mouthwatering pastries (middle); maple syrup, an ideal souvenir (bottom)

MUSEUM STORES

When you are searching for souvenirs and gifts, don't overlook the stores within museums and art galleries, which generally stock high quality, authentic arts, crafts and design, wonderful books and posters, and sometimes clothing. Particularly good ones include the Musée des Beaux-Arts (▷ 54), the Musée d'Art Contemporain (▷ 51), Pointe-à-Callière (▷ 30, 41) and Musée McCord d'Histoire Canadienne (▷ 55).

Shopping by Theme

Whether you're looking for a department store, a quirky boutique, or something in between, you'll find it all in Montréal. On this page shops are listed by theme. For a more detailed write-up, see the individual listings in Montréal by Area.

Montréal by Night

Montréalers never hibernate, no matter how cold it gets. Saturday-night crowds are almost as large in January as they are in July.

Hot Spots
Downtown, the scene is mainly on four streets that run between boulevard René-Lévesque and rue Sherbrooke—de la Montagne, Crescent, Bishop and Mackay. They're lined with fine old graystone residences now converted into pubs, clubs and bistros, which appeal to a young, hip and largely English speaking crowd. Just as vibrant but more French in ambience is the district around the twin corridors of boulevard Saint-Laurent and rue Saint-Denis. Start around rue Sainte-Catherine and walk away from the river through the Quartier Latin and Plateau Mont-Royal, exploring the cafés and clubs on Prince-Arthur and Rachel. Petite Italie is also buzzing after dark, while Le Village is the focus of the gay scene. There's plenty of entertainment in Montréal for all ages and you'll find both languages spoken everywhere.

Evening Stroll
Vieux-Montréal has only a few nightclubs, but it's a wonderful place for an evening stroll. Many of the old classical buildings, including the Hôtel de Ville, Place Royale and Château Ramezay, are beautifully illuminated, and a small section of rue Sainte-Hélène is evocatively lit by gas lamps.

LONG HISTORY
Montréal has been a popular hot spot with Americans since at least the 1920s and 1930s. During Prohibition, trainloads of fun-seekers from New York and Boston would pour into the city every weekend looking for some excitement and a little legal booze. The city was also popular with African-American jazz musicians, who liked the fact they could pretty much stay and eat wherever they wanted—and date locals without raising so much as an eyebrow.

Party all night at a club, try your luck in a casino, go to rue Ste-Catherine, visit the ballet, or take in some jazz

13

Eating Out

Montréal is one of North America's gastronomic capitals, a city that is passionate about its food, and that draws on French and other ethnic culinary influences to offer a wonderfully rich assortment of restaurants, cafés and cuisines.

French Tastes
France is the obvious point of culinary reference, and French-influenced food is the city's most widespread, found not only in restaurants that wouldn't be out of place in Paris, but also in a plethora of cafés and bistros in settings every bit as Gallic as their European counterparts.

Plenty of Choice
The city's rich and multicultural population provides the inspiration for countless other cuisines—from Thai, Vietnamese and Korean to Indian, Chinese and Italian. Not forgetting the classic staples of North America, with some excellent steak houses, plenty of places for pasta, chicken and seafood, and delis for bagels and cured meats.

Where to Go
The key dining areas are well defined, the most popular being rue Saint-Denis and boulevard Saint-Laurent beyond rue Sherbrooke. Here, as in Vieux-Montréal, you are spoiled for choice, though the downtown area, too, has plenty to offer. Also, explore Le Village, the Plateau, Mile End, western rue Notre-Dame and Petite Italie.

PRACTICALITIES

At lunch, look out for set-price two- or three-course menus known as the *spécial du midi,* or midday special. These are good value, as are the two- to four-course set *table d'hôte* menus in the evening. These menus will usually be better value than eating à la carte. A multi-course *menu dégustacion,* or tasting menu, will be expensive, but will offer a selection of dishes in small portions, often accompanied by different wines. A starter, or appetizer, in Montréal is called an *entrée,* and the main course is the *plat principal.*

In a city very much influenced by the French, expect to find many atmospheric street cafés and bistros

Restaurants by Cuisine

There are restaurants to suit all tastes and budgets in Montréal. On this page they are listed by cuisine. For a more detailed description of each restaurant, see Montréal by Area.

BREAKFAST/BRUNCH

Dans la Bouche (▷ 81)
Première Moisson
   (▷ 106)
Quoi de n'Oeufs
   (▷ 106)

CAFÉS/PÂTISSERIES

La Brioche Lyonnaise
   (▷ 81)
Café Santropol (▷ 81)
Café Bistro (▷ 65)
Code Ambiance (▷ 65)
La Concession (▷ 43)
Olive et Gourmando
   (▷ 44)
Pasticceria Alati-Caserta
   (▷ 106)
Presse Café (▷ 66)

CONTEMPORARY

Beaver Hall (▷ 65)
Bistrot La Fabrique
   (▷ 81)
Brutopia (▷ 65)
Chez L'Épicier (▷ 43)
The Hambar (▷ 44)
Le Local (▷ 44)
Toque! (▷ 44)

ETHNIC CUISINE

Café Ferreira (▷ 81)
Café Stash (▷ 43)
Gandhi (▷ 44)
Limon (▷ 106)
Le Taj (▷ 66)
Phaya Thai (▷ 82)

FRENCH

À La Découverte (▷ 81)
Ariel (▷ 65)
Au Bistro Gourmet
   (▷ 65)
Auberge le Saint-Gabriel
   (▷ 43)
Beaver Club (▷ 65)
Bonaparte (▷ 43)
Boris Bistro (▷ 43)
Club Chasse et Peche
   (▷ 44)
L'Express (▷ 81)
Laloux (▷ 82)
Le Mas des Oliviers
   (▷ 66)
Scena (▷ 44)

MEDITERRANEAN

Andiamo (▷ 65)
Da Emma (▷ 44)
Graziella (▷ 44)
Le Jardin de Panos
   (▷ 82)
L'Omnivore (▷ 82)
Pizzaria Geppetto
   (▷ 106)
Pizzaria Napoletana
   (▷ 106)
Psarotaverna du
   Symposium (▷ 82)

PAN-ASIAN CUISINE

Bon Blé Riz (▷ 81)
Maiko Sushi (▷ 82)
La Maison V.I.P. (▷ 66)
Orchidée de Chine
   (▷ 66)
Ruby Rouge (▷ 66)

Shu Shian Yuang (▷ 82)
Tatami (▷ 44)

STEAK AND FISH

Au Pied de Cochon
   (▷ 81)
Le Bourlingueur (▷ 43)
L'Entrecôte Saint-Jean
   (▷ 66)
Joe Beef (▷ 106)
Liverpool House
   (▷ 106)
m:brgr (▷ 66)
Moishe's (▷ 82)
Mr. Steer (▷ 66)
Schwartz's (▷ 82)
Uniburger (▷ 82)

Top Tips For...

However you'd like to spend your time in Montréal, these top suggestions should help you tailor your ideal visit. Each suggestion has a fuller write-up elsewhere in the book.

BURNING THE MIDNIGHT OIL

Board a night-time cruise with disco on the Saint Lawrence river (▷ 33).
Visit the clubs of the Quartier Latin (▷ 80).
Join the revelers in one of downtown's Irish bars, including Pub Le Vieux Dublin (▷ 64), with its live Celtic music nights.

THE LAP OF LUXURY

Stay on the "Gold Floor" of the Fairmont Le Reine Elizabeth hotel (▷ 112).
Eat at Toque!, one of the city's finest restaurants (▷ 44).
Go mad among the designer labels showcased in the designer shops on avenue Laurier at the north end of Parc du Mont-Royal (▷ 72–73).

TO KEEP YOUR CHILDREN HAPPY

Take them to a performance at TOHU (▷ 105).
Strap them in for a jet-boat trip over the Lachine Rapids (▷ 33).
Visit the Insectarium and Biodôme (▷ 86) at the Parc Olympique (▷ 91).

SAVING MONEY

Go to the visitor center in rue Peel (▷ 119) for details of free concerts in churches, parks, malls and the Vieux-Port.
Remember that some museums in Montréal have free entry on certain days and nights.
Summer festivals such as *Juste Pour Rire* (Just for Laughs) and the International Jazz Festival have many free events (▷ 114).

Downtown gets lively after dark (above); powerboat rafting (middle); jazz features at many of the summer festivals (bottom)

Nightlife at the Sky Pub (below); Nelligan Hotel, old Montreal(below middle)

AN EVENING OF ENTERTAINMENT

Attend an ice-hockey game involving Les Canadiens (▷ 64, Centre Bell).
The place des Arts plays host to several orchestras and leading ballet and opera companies (▷ 64).
Listen to jazz at Quai des Brumes (▷ 80), where there are two very different jazz clubs in one building.

A MEMORABLE PLACE TO STAY

For modern chic and contemporary styling, the Hôtel (10) and "W" hotel win hands down (▷ 112).
The Hôtel Nelligan is divinely romantic (▷ 112).
Inexpensive, central and intimate, the Auberge de la place Royale is a quirky gem (▷ 110).

ROMANTIC SUPPERS

The Quartier Latin has numerous romantic little bistros (▷ 81–82).
In summer, Boris Bistro's lovely terrace is the place to eat (▷ 43).
Beaver Club (▷ 65) is one of the city's most sumptuous dining rooms.

A typically stylish room at one of Montréal's many chic hotels

A TASTE OF TRADITION

Steaks at Moishe's have been aged and prepared the same way since 1938 (▷ 82).

Classic smoked and cured meats are the specialty of old-world Schwartz's (▷ 82).
Grab a late-night snack at one of Montréal's famous bagel bakeries (▷ 78, 79). They never close.

Popular bagel shop in Montreal

ESSENTIAL MONTRÉAL TOP TIPS FOR...

A BREATH OF FRESH AIR

Clamber to the heights of the Parc du Mont-Royal (▷ 72).

Take a turn around the Jardin Botanique (▷ 88), adjoining Parc Maisonneuve (▷ 94).

Enjoy a brisk stroll along the Lachine Canal (▷ 98).

Savor the Montréal skyline from high spots around the city

SHOPPING UNDER ONE ROOF

La Baie (▷ 62) and Ogilvy (▷ 62) are landmark downtown department stores.

Les Promenades Cathédrale (▷ 63) is a five-layer mall.

The Underground City is a labyrinth of shops sheltered from the elements (▷ 57).

SPECIALTY SHOPPING

Marché Bonsecours (▷ 28) and nearby rue Saint-Paul (▷ 31) are excellent for traditional art, craft and design.

Explore rue Saint-Denis for cutting-edge clothes and funky stores (▷ 76).

Rue Amherst near rue Ontario and rue Notre-Dame Ouest near rue Guy are great for antiques and retro decor (▷ 79).

CUTTING-EDGE CULTURE

Fine arts and a fine setting define the Musée des Beaux-Arts (▷ 54).

Be shocked or amused but never bored at the Musée d'Art Contemporain (▷ 51)— and don't forget its sculpture garden.

Pointe-à-Callière offers Montréal's best interactive history museum (▷ 30).

A maze of shops all linked together by Montréal's Underground City (above)

The abstract facade of the Musée des Beaux-Arts, the oldest museum in the country

Montréal by Area

Once the heart of the ancient city, Vieux-Montréal has been transformed into a busy and revitalized area.

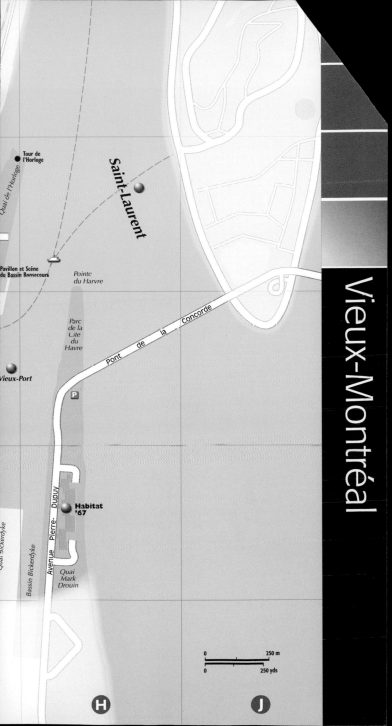

Tour de
l'Horloge

Quai de l'Horloge

Saint-Laurent

Pavillon et Scéne
du Bassin Bonsecours

Pointe
du Harvre

Pont de la Concorde

Parc
de la
Cité
du
Havre

Vieux-Port

P

Avenue Pierre- Dupuy

Habitat
'67

Quai Bickerdyke

Bassin Bickerdyke

Quai
Mark
Drouin

Vieux-Montréal

| 0 | | 250 m |
| 0 | | 250 yds |

H   J

HIGHLIGHTS

● Pulpit
● Wood carving
● Stained glass
● High altar

TIPS

● No more than an hour is needed for a visit.
● Son et Lumière shows take place Tue–Thu (usually at 6.30pm) and twice on Fri (6.30 and 8.30pm) and Sat (7 and 8.30pm). Cost is $10 and tickets are from the "Parvis" shop in the church.

No other site in Montréal sums up the city's religious heritage as beautifully as the Basilica of Notre-Dame, where the seductive interior—Romanesque with touches of rococo—lifts you into a world of almost perfect calm.

History Founded in 1657, Notre-Dame is on the flanks of place d'Armes, the historic focus of the old city. The original church was replaced by the present neo-Gothic basilica between 1824 and 1829. Today there is a skyscraper on the square's western side, but the church's twin towers—nicknamed Temperance and Perseverance—still command the skyline. The western tower, built in 1843, contains the famous "Gros Bourdon" bell; the bell's peal can be heard up to 25km (15 miles) away.

A horse-drawn carriage (caleche) pulls up outside the Basilique Notre-Dame (left); an illuminated backdrop highlights the basilica's ornate altar (right)

Highly decorated Inside, thousands of tiny 24-carat gold stars stud the dusky blue, vaulted ceiling, and 14 stained-glass windows, brought from Limoges in 1929, tell the story of Ville-Marie's early development. But most of the interior is a tribute to the woodworking skills of Québec artists and artisans. All the figures in the life-size tableaus behind the main altar are carved in wood, as is the spectacular pulpit with its curving staircase on the east side of the nave. A fire in 1978 destroyed much of the large chapel behind the main altar. The Sulpician priests who run the church saved what they could of the woodwork and erected an enormous, modern bronze sculpture behind the altar. The chapel is still the most popular for weddings in Montréal; in 1994 singer Céline Dion married her manager here in a ceremony that rivaled the pomp of a royal wedding.

THE BASICS

www.basiliquenddm.org

✚ F11

✉ 110 rue Notre-Dame Ouest

☎ Basilica 514/842-2925

🕐 Mon–Fri 8–4.30, Sat 8–4, Sun 12.30–4

🚇 Place d'Armes

🚌 38, 55, 129

♿ Very good

💲 Inexpensive

❓ 20-min guided tours in French or English daily included in ticket price. Sound and light show Tue–Sat ($10)

25

The Centre d'Histoire de Montréal is on place d'Youville (left); a display inside (right)

VIEUX-MONTRÉAL TOP 25

THE BASICS

www.ville.montreal.qc.ca

✚ F12

✉ 335 place d'Youville

☎ 514/872-3207

◷ Tue–Sun 10–5

Ⓡ Square-Victoria, Place d'Armes

🚌 14, 55, 129

♿ Moderate

❓ Guided tours need to be arranged in advance

HIGHLIGHTS

● Fire Station building
● Tram car
● Youville Stables

Although this history museum seems a little dated at first glance, it tells Montréal's story in an interesting way, allowing you to step in and share snippets of Montréalers' day-to-day lives from 1642 to the present.

History Of the monuments and historic sites that line place d'Youville, one of Montréal's earliest market squares, the most attractive is the beautifully restored red-stone Caserne Centrale de Pompiers, or old Central Fire Station (1903). Today this building houses the Centre d'Histoire de Montréal, an 11-room interpretative center, which uses dioramas, videos and other media to trace the city's development from Iroquois settlement to metropolis. Look for the mock-ups of the streetcar, the 19th-century factory and the gaudy 1940s living room. Temporary exhibitions on off-beat aspects of the city's history are held upstairs.

Also on the square On the square's south side are the Youville Stables (Écuries d'Youville), graystone buildings constructed in 1828 as ware-houses for grain merchants and soap manufac-turers (the stables were next door). In 1967 the complex was converted into offices, shops and artisans' studios. Just off the square a plaque com-memorates the Hôpital Général des Sœurs-Grises (Gray Nuns' General Hospital), founded in 1694 and taken over in 1747 by Marguerite d'Youville, the widow who founded the Sœurs Grises. The order treated the sick, poor and elderly and estab-lished one of the first foundling hospitals.

Glorious statues adorn the Chapelle Notre-Dame-de-Bon-Secours, inside and out

Chapelle Notre-Dame-de-Bon-Secours

This tiny building is a monument to Marguerite Bourgeoys, a pious woman dedicated to bringing Christian civilization to New France. She founded a religious order, set up schools and built this church.

Chapel St. Marguerite Bourgeoys picked the site for the chapel in 1657, just outside Ville-Marie's stockade. She persuaded Montréal's founder, Paul de Chomedey, Sieur de Maisonneuve, to help with the project. The original building was destroyed by fire, and the present stone edifice dates from 1771. The 1998 renovation revealed some beautiful 18th-century murals.

A sailors' haunt The chapel has always had a special place in the hearts of mariners. Situated on the waterfront, it was built to house a small 17th-century statue of Notre-Dame-de-Bon-Secours (Our Lady of Good Hope), credited with the rescue of those in peril at sea. A larger-than-life statue of the Virgin graces the steeple of the present building, facing the river with arms outstretched in welcome. Mariners who survived ocean crossings in the 18th and 19th centuries often came to the church to thank the Virgin for her help, and to leave votive lamps in the shape of small model ships. Many of them still hang from the ceiling and the chapel is usually referred to simply as the Église des Matelots, the Sailors' Church. Visitors can climb the steeple to the "Aerial," a tiny chapel where mariners came to pray. In the museum you can learn about St. Marguerite Bourgeoys.

THE BASICS

www.marguerite-bourgeoys.com

⊞ G10

✉ 400 rue Saint-Paul Est

☎ 514/282-8670

🕐 May to mid-Oct Tue–Sun 10–6; Nov to mid-Jan, Mar–Apr Tue–Sun 11–4

🚇 Champ-de-Mars

🚌 14, 129

♿ Poor: four steps to church; no access to tower or museum

💵 Chapel free. Museum moderate

❓ Small gift shop. Guided tours of crypt archaeological site (includes museum entry) $12

HIGHLIGHTS

- Gold Madonna
- Murals
- Votive boats
- Mosaic inlays
- Madonna de Bon-Secours
- "Aerial"
- Views

VIEUX-MONTRÉAL TOP 25

Marché Bonsecours

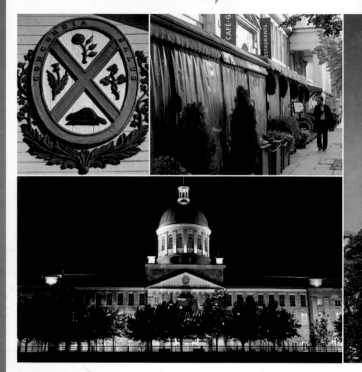

HIGHLIGHTS

● Silver dome
● Facade and portico
● Shopping

TIPS

● For coffee, sandwiches, snacks and light meals visit Le Petit Paysan inside the market.
● The Quebec Craft Council's Boutique des Métiers d'Art (▷ 40) is one of the 15 stores and galleries specializing in high-quality art and design items.

The silvery dome of the Marché Bonsecours has been a landmark on the Montréal waterfront for well over a century. It serves as a reminder of the city's importance as a busy port during the 19th century.

In the beginning The site of the Marché Bonsecours was important in 18th-century New France. Colonial authorities had an administrative center here and the Marché Neuf, built to replace Montréal's first market in Place Royale, was nearby. The present building was never meant to serve as a market. The British erected it between 1845 and 1850 to fill cultural and political needs: The city councillors met downstairs and musicians played in the concert hall upstairs. It was only in 1878, when the mayor and city legislators

The Marché Bonsecours began life as a concert hall and a meeting place for city councillors; now it's a shopping arcade

moved to their new home on rue Notre-Dame, that it became a market and remained so until the early 1960s. After redevelopment, the building served again as municipal offices until May 1996, when it reopened as a shopping arcade.

Today The present graystone building is one of the most graceful in the city. Its long neoclassical facade, punctuated by rows of white-painted sash windows, stretches for two blocks. The main portico, supported by six cast-iron Doric columns, fronts on cobbled rue Saint-Paul in the heart of the old city. Artists and artisans display their wares in shops and stalls on the lower level and the upper floor is used for temporary exhibitions, and for concerts and banquets. The back door opens on the Vieux-Port (▷ 32). In summer there is an outdoor café at street level.

THE BASICS

www.marchebonsecours.qc.ca

✚ G10

✉ 350 rue Saint-Paul Est at rue Bonsecours

☎ 514/872-7730

🕐 Jan–Mar daily 10–6; Apr–late Jun and Nov–Dec Sat–Wed 10–6, Thu–Fri 10–9; late Jun–Labor Day daily 10–9; Labor Day–Oct Sun–Wed 10–6, Thu–Sat 10–9

🚇 Champ-de-Mars

🚌 14

♿ Very good

💲 Free

Pointe-à-Callière

Musée d'Archéologie et d'Histoire de Montréal has put Pointe-à-Callière well and truly on the map

HIGHLIGHTS

- Archaeological site
- Pirates or Privateers?
- Youville Pumping Station
- Where Montréal Was Born
- Multimedia Show

TIPS

- Allow 1–2 hours for a visit.
- Admission includes free 20- or 60-minute guided tours (Tue–Sun only) in French and English.

Of all the innovations in the Vieux-Port, the superb Musée d'Archéologie et d'Histoire de Montréal at Pointe-à-Callière is the most impressive. It is the best of the developments that have given a little heart to old Montréal.

Archaeology and history Visit this magnificent museum on your first morning in Montréal: It provides a fascinating introduction to the city's history, and it is also built at Pointe-à-Callière, where Montréal's first 53 settlers landed from France on May 17, 1642. The museum uses audiovisual displays to tell the story of Montréal's development as a trading and meeting place.

Underground The main building of this $27-million museum is the stark, shiplike Édifice de l'Eperon, built on the foundations of the Royal Insurance building. It houses offices, temporary exhibits, a café with river views, and a theater with a 16-minute multimedia show on Montréal's history. But its real treasures are underground. The museum gives access to the excavations underneath, where archaeologists have burrowed into the silt and rock to expose the remains of a 19th-century sewer system, 18th-century tavern foundations and a cemetery dating to 1643. As you explore, you have virtual encounters with some of the city's more colorful citizens. Tunnels connect the excavations to the Old Customs House, where there are more exhibits. The museum also incorporates the Youville Pumping Station, the city's first electrical wastewater-pumping system.

Rue Saint-Paul

This narrow, cobblestone street is the picturesque main thoroughfare of Vieux-Montréal and dates from the origins of the city. Today its old buildings offer an enticing mix of art and craft galleries, boutiques and restaurants.

Historic origins Most of the old buildings that line the street date from the 19th and early 20th century and are a pleasing mix of stone and brick. The clever use of street lighting to highlight the architectural features makes an after-dark stroll doubly worthwhile. Daytime attractions include the fabulous Marché Bonsecours (▷ 28), the Chapelle Notre-Dame-de-Bon-Secours, with its Musée Marguerite-Bourgeoys (▷ 27), and the beautifully restored Maison Papineau (▷ 36), all clustered around the intersection with rue Bonsecours. Another building of particular interest is the Hostellerie Pierre du Calvet, now a chic bed-and-breakfast.

Vibrant street The real joy of rue Saint-Paul, though, is just to wander, explore the galleries and stores and soak up the atmosphere—particularly buzzing after dark or during any of the festivals based here or on the waterfront, which runs parallel. It's also fun to join the locals on the roof terrace of the chic Hôtel Nelligan (▷ 112), a prime city spot for *cinq a sept* (5–7pm), the traditional Montréal after-work get-together. You can also hop over one street to the waterfront quays of the Vieux-Port (▷ 32), where there are facilities for many activities.

THE BASICS

✚ G11
🚇 Champ de Mars, Place d'Armes
🚌 55, 129

HIGHLIGHTS

● Marché Bonsecours
● The commercial art galleries
● A caleche ride (from place d'Armes)
● Bar-hopping after dark

VIEUX-MONTRÉAL TOP 25

Vieux-Port

Bassin Bonsecours, Prom du Vieux-Port

THE BASICS

www.oldportofmontreal.com

www.vieux-montreal.qu.ca

G11

Access from points along rue de la Commune and rue Berri

514/496-7678 or 800/971-7678

On Place Jacques-Cartier and elsewhere

Place d'Armes, Champ-de-Mars, Square-Victoria

55, 75, 715

Free but fees for most attractions and ice rink

HIGHLIGHTS

- Centre des Sciences
- Labyrinthe du Hangar 16
- Centre d'Histoire de Montréal
- Tour de l'Horloge
- Multimedia Show

TIPS

- Check the Old Port website for special offers.
- Free WiFi is available through most of the Old Port Area

The Old Port was the heart of the city from its earliest days, home to the quays that received the first pioneers. The port was moved in 1976 and the area revitalized in the 1990s to create a dynamic waterfront that stretches for over a mile (2km) along the Saint Lawrence.

Leisure activities Attractions are divided between the park area set back from the water and the various old docks and piers and their converted warehouses. Among other things, the latter contain the Centre des Sciences de Montréal (▷ 33) and Labyrinthe du Hangar 16 (▷ 35), as well as providing the point of embarkation for many of the boat trips up and down the Saint Lawrence River (▷ 33). The waterfront park area is a pleasure to wander for its own sake, with plenty of trails, cafés and restaurants, most with outdoor terraces. You can also rent bikes, inline skates, pleasure boats and Segways to explore both this area and farther afield along the Lachine Canal at the port's eastern end.

Festivals In summer you'll always find a festival of some sort in progress, as well as street performers and bigger shows. In 2012 an urban beach was created near the Tour de l'Horloge (clock tower), begun in 1919 as a memorial to Canadian sailors who died in World War I: climb the tower for some fine views. Winter, too, has its festivals, along the with chance tro go ice fishing and join the locals skating on a large ice rink between December and early March.

BANQUE DE MONTRÉAL

Canada's oldest financial institution was founded in 1817. Thirty years later its headquarters moved to this neoclassical building inspired by Rome's Pantheon. The bank's small museum displays coins, mechanical piggy banks and a check written on a beaver pelt.

🛉 F11 ✉ 129 rue Saint-Jacques ☎ 514/877-6810 🕘 Mon–Fri 9–4 🚇 Place d'Armes 🦽 Good 🎟 Free

BOAT TRIPS ON THE SAINT LAWRENCE RIVER

The Saint Lawrence (Saint-Laurent) has been Montréal's lifeblood, a vital artery for trade and communication, for centuries. You can enjoy a taste of the great river on one of the short cruises or thrilling jet boats that leave from the Vieux-Port. Daytime and evening cruises are available, including dinner and entertainment cruises. Most offer views of the port area and islands of Notre-Dame and Sainte-Hélène, while a few venture farther afield to the Commune, Sainte-Marguerite and other islands beyond Longueuil.

🛉 G10/G11 🚇 Champ-de-Mars, Place d'Armes 🚌 55, 129

Le Bateau Mouche
✉ Quai Jacques-Cartier ☎ 514/849-9952; www.bateaumouche.ca

Saute Moutons
✉ Quai de l'Horloge ☎ 514/284-9607; www.jetboatingmontreal.com

Croisières AML
✉ Quai King Edward ☎ 866/856-6668; www.croisieresaml.com

CENTRE DES SCIENCES DE MONTRÉAL

www.montrealsciencecentre.com

On one of the quays of the Vieux-Port, this excellent science museum underwent a complete redevelopment in 2007 and reopened with even more exciting exhibits and interactive displays. It ranges from basic scientific concepts to the impact of science and technology on our daily lives, offers glimpses into the future and explores

View of the Biosphère from a Bateau Mouche

Banque de Montréal

VIEUX-MONTRÉAL | MORE TO SEE

...sues. There's ...ity to create, edit and present your own TV news segment and learn about the latest Canadian inventions and innovations. Sharing the building is an IMAX movie theater.

⊞ G11 ⊠ King Edward Pier, rue de la Commune ☎ 514/496-4724 or 877/496-4724 🕐 Mon–Fri 9–4, Sat–Sun 10–5 Ⓜ Place d'Armes 🚌 14, 55, 129 🍴 Café Arsenik 💵 Expensive; combined tickets with IMAX available

CHÂTEAU RAMEZAY

www.chateauramezay.qc.ca

French governors, British conquerors and American generals have all stayed in this relic of the French regime. With its squat round towers and its rough stone finish, Château Ramezay is like a piece of Normandy in North America.

One of North America's most venerable buildings, this country house was commissioned in 1705 by Claude de Ramezay, 11th Governor of Montréal, and was the work of master mason Pierre Couturier, one of the leading architects of his day (the distinctive round tower was a 19th-century addition, however).

In 1745 de Ramezay's heir sold it to governors of the Compagnie des Indes (West Indies Company), which had the monopoly on beaver pelts sold in French North America until the British arrived. Under the French the house became Montréal's most fashionable meeting place.

After 1763 the building was home to the Governors General of British North America, and during the brief American invasion of 1775 served as a military headquarters for American commanders Benedict Arnold and Richard Montgomery. Benjamin Franklin came later the same year in a doomed attempt to persuade Montréalers to join the US.

In 1895 the house was bought and turned into a museum, its interior fitted and furnished as

The Château Ramezay is a reminder of Normandy in North America

it might have been in the 18th century with paintings, costumes and furniture. The kitchen, one of the most appealing parts of the house, is filled with period utensils. The intricate carving of the wood-paneled Grande Salle is a reminder of the opulence of 18th-century Montréal. This is more than a furnished historic house, though, with museum collections amounting to some 30,000 objects—fine arts, First Nations and colonial items, numismatics, photographs and a library. The gardens are dotted with information panels and often host special events.

➕ G10 ✉ 280 rue Notre-Dame Est at rue Saint-Claude ☎ 514/861-3708 🕐 Jun to mid-Oct daily 10–6; mid-Oct to May Tue–Sun 10–4.30 🚇 Champ-de-Mars 🚌 14, 129 💰 Moderate

ÉDIFICE ALDRED

The Aldred Building (1928) is celebrated for its art deco features.

➕ F11 ✉ 501–507 place d'Armes 🚇 Place d'Armes

HABITAT '67

Habitat '67 is a modern housing development designed for Expo '67 by Moshe Safdie, one of Montréal's leading architects. Safdie was disillusioned with suburbia and most public housing, especially high-rise developments, which he felt cut people off from open spaces and the amenities of the city. His project here was an attempt to build better housing more cheaply by mass-producing much of each housing unit in factories and then delivering them ready-made to the buildings' site. From afar, the project, with its cubist houses stacked on top of one another, looks strange and impressive but Montréalers never really took to the dull concrete exteriors and inadequately protected pedestrian streets, and in 1986 the government sold the complex to its residents for just half the initial cost of $22 million.

➕ H12 ✉ Avenue Pierre-Dupuy, Cité du Havre 🚌 168

The strange box-like residential block (Habitat '67) built for the Expo '67

LABYRINTHE DU HANGAR 16

www.vieux-montreal.qc.ca

This indoor maze challenges children to hunt for clues while finding their way through the labyrinth. There's a different themed mystery to solve each year, in addition to specials such as a spooky Halloween event.

➕ G10 ✉ Quai de l'Horloge, Vieux-Port ☎ 514/499-0099 ⏲ Mid-May to mid-Jun and Sep daily 11.30–5.30; Jun 24–Aug 27 11–9 Ⓜ Champ-de-Mars 👋 Expensive

LIEU HISTORIQUE NATIONAL SIR GEORGE-ÉTIENNE CARTIER

www.pc.gc.ca/lhn-nhs/qc/etiennecartier.aspx

Sir George-Étienne Cartier, once a leading rebel against British rule, was later to become one of the founding fathers of the Canadian confederation, persuading the French Canadians that a united Canada was the way forward. This museum occupies two connected houses that were home to the Cartier family between 1848 and 1872. One has displays explaining Cartier's political and industrial pre-occupations (he was a lawyer and the Grand Trunk Railway was one of his clients), while the other portrays his family life, complete with many original pieces of furniture and other domestic objects.

➕ G10 ✉ 458 rue Notre-Dame Est, corner of rue Berri ☎ 514/283-2282 or 888/773-8888 ⏲ Early Jun to early Sep daily 10–5; early Apr to early Jun, early Sep to Dec 23 Fri–Sun, public hols 10–5 Ⓜ Champ-de-Mars 🚌 14, 239 👋 Inexpensive; theatrical presentations moderate ❓ Guided tours

MAISON PAPINEAU

This beautiful house was built by John Campbell, a colonel in the British army, who is said to have purchased the land from Joseph Papineau, the grandfather of Louis-Joseph Papineau (1786–1871), one of the great political figures in the French-Canadian nationalist movement. Campbell's widow then sold the house to Louis-Joseph's father. He then in turn left it to Louis-Joseph, and it remained in

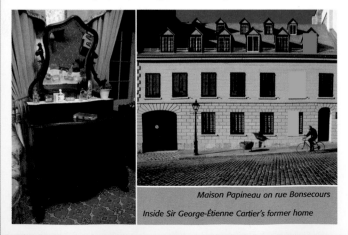

Maison Papineau on rue Bonsecours

Inside Sir George-Étienne Cartier's former home

the family until 1964. Today, it is owned by the Canadian government. The house has been restored to its splendid 1830s appearance as a memorial to Papineau.

➕ G10 ✉ 440 rue Bonsecours ☎ None 🕐 Exterior only 🚇 Champ-de-Mars ♿ On a sloping, cobbled street

MAISON PIERRE-DU-CALVET

A fine 18th-century house built in 1770 for merchant Pierre du Calvet. Note the thick walls and fireplaces, and the windows with little squares of glass.

➕ G10 ✉ 401 rue Bonsecours ☎ 514/282-1725 🚇 Champ-de-Mars

PLACE D'ARMES

Place d'Armes was laid out at the end of the 17th century around the main source of drinking water for the first French settlement. In the center is a statue (1895) of Paul de Chomedey, Montréal's founder, Sieur de Maisonneuve. Around it are Basilique Notre-Dame (▷ 24–25), Montréal's oldest building, the Séminaire de Saint-Sulpice, the Banque de Montréal (▷ 33), the Aldred Building (▷ 35) and the eight-floor Édifice New York Life (1888). This is also the place to hire a horse-drawn caleche and driver for a tour of Vieux-Montréal. The place d'Armes is scheduled for a facelift in the near future. Montréal is a UNESCO City of Design and its fellow cities on the list are being asked to participate in the redesign process.

➕ F11 🚇 Place d'Armes

PLACE JACQUES-CARTIER

Right in the heart of Vieux-Montréal, this lovely cobbled square was created in 1804 as a municipal market; now its cafés, musicians, restaurants and quaint shops draw lively summer crowds. Nelson's Column is here and there are several fine 19th-century houses, including the Maison del Vecchio, Maison Cartier and Maison Vandelac.

➕ G10 🚇 Champ-de-Mars

Place d'Armes

Place Jacques-Cartier

PLACE ROYALE

Place Royale is Montréal's oldest square, and has a history that stretches back to when the area's aboriginal population occupied the site. Artifacts suggest the area has been continually inhabited for at least 2,000 years. For a period in the 17th century the site was used for an annual fur-trading market. Thus was born the industry that would be the basis of Montréal's wealth for decades. In 1701, the French and aboriginal peoples signed a treaty here that brought an end to their wars. In later years the square was the site of public punishments, and was known then as Customs Square. It took its present name in 1892.

➕ F11 🚇 Place d'Armes

PLACE D'YOUVILLE

The fish market and dried-up creek are long gone, and what we see today is a public space that has been imaginatively landscaped. Though the western part is still a parking lot, there are plans for an overhaul here too.

➕ F12 🚇 Square-Victoria

RUE BONSECOURS

A good example of the classical ideals of Montréal's early French planners, with fine homes. Look for No. 401 Maison Pierre-du-Calvet (▷ 37) and No. 440 Maison Papineau (▷ 36).

➕ G10 🚇 Champ-de-Mars

RUE SAINT-AMABLE

This narrow and lively cobbled alley off place Jacques-Cartier is notorious for the many portrait artists vying for business amid the throng.

➕ G11 🚇 Place d'Armes

VIEUX PALAIS DE JUSTICE

This impressive neoclassical courthouse (1856) heard civil cases for almost a century. Most of it is now municipal offices, but you can admire the dome and portico.

➕ F10 ✉ 155 rue Notre-Dame Est
🚇 Champ-de-Mars

Vieux Palais de Justice　　*Maison Pierre du Calvet, rue Bonsecours*

Vieux-Montréal

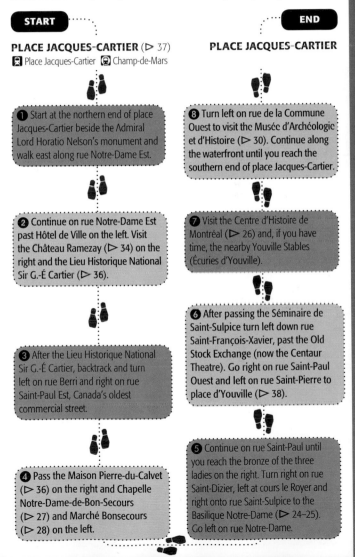

This easy walk takes you along the main streets and past the key churches, monuments, squares and civic buildings of Old Montréal.

DISTANCE: 3km (2 miles) **ALLOW:** 2–6 hours depending on sights visited

START

PLACE JACQUES-CARTIER (▷ 37)
🚇 Place Jacques-Cartier 🚇 Champ-de-Mars

END

PLACE JACQUES-CARTIER

1 Start at the northern end of place Jacques-Cartier beside the Admiral Lord Horatio Nelson's monument and walk east along rue Notre-Dame Est.

2 Continue on rue Notre-Dame Est past Hôtel de Ville on the left. Visit the Château Ramezay (▷ 34) on the right and the Lieu Historique National Sir G.-É Cartier (▷ 36).

3 After the Lieu Historique National Sir G.-É Cartier, backtrack and turn left on rue Berri and right on rue Saint-Paul Est, Canada's oldest commercial street.

4 Pass the Maison Pierre-du-Calvet (▷ 36) on the right and Chapelle Notre-Dame-de-Bon-Secours (▷ 27) and Marché Bonsecours (▷ 28) on the left.

8 Turn left on rue de la Commune Ouest to visit the Musée d'Archéologie et d'Histoire (▷ 30). Continue along the waterfront until you reach the southern end of place Jacques-Cartier.

7 Visit the Centre d'Histoire de Montréal (▷ 26) and, if you have time, the nearby Youville Stables (Écuries d'Youville).

6 After passing the Séminaire de Saint-Sulpice turn left down rue Saint-François-Xavier, past the Old Stock Exchange (now the Centaur Theatre). Go right on rue Saint-Paul Ouest and left on rue Saint-Pierre to place d'Youville (▷ 38).

5 Continue on rue Saint-Paul until you reach the bronze of the three ladies on the right. Turn right on rue Saint-Dizier, left at cours le Royer and right onto rue Saint-Sulpice to the Basilique Notre-Dame (▷ 24–25). Go left on rue Notre-Dame.

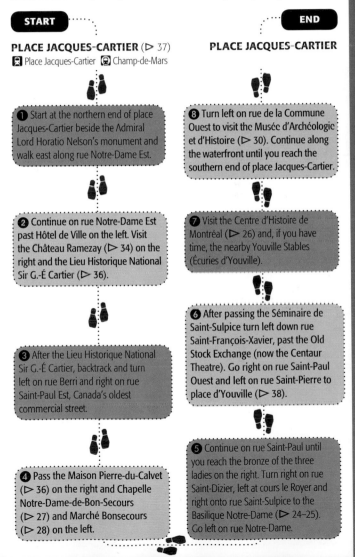

VIEUX-MONTRÉAL WALK

Shopping

ART ET COMPAGNIE
www.artetcie.ca
Provides a showcase for local and regional artists and craftspeople, and is a good place to pick up slightly out-of-the-ordinary souvenirs.
⊞ G10 ✉ 347 rue Saint-Paul Est ☎ 514/564-9990 🕔 Mon–Wed 12–5, Thu–Fri 12–9, Sat 11–6, Sun 12–6 🚇 Champ-de-Mars

CANADIAN MAPLE DELIGHTS
www.mapledelights.com
Mouthwatering aromas are overwhelming in this shop and bistro, where you can sample or buy a wide range of maple syrup-based products, including some superb pastries and delicious ice creams.
⊞ G11 ✉ 84 rue Saint-Paul Est ☎ 514/765-3456, Ext 224 🕔 Mon–Thu 9–7, Fri 9–9, Sat 10–9, Sun 10–7 🚇 Champ-de-Mars

L'EMPREINTE COOPÉRATIVE
www.lempreintecoop.com
A dazzling store that showcases the work of numerous craftspeople from across the province of Québec.
⊞ G10 ✉ 88 rue Saint-Paul Est ☎ 514/861-4427 🕔 Daily 11–6 🚇 Place d'Armes

GALERIE LE CHARIOT
www.galeriesmontreal.ca
A piece of Inuit or other aboriginal art is one of the most distinctive

and purely Canadian of souvenirs. This gallery has one of Canada's largest collections of soapstone, ivory, jade and other Inuit carvings, as well as numerous other high-quality works of art. Prices, though, are correspondingly high.
⊞ F11 ✉ 446 place Jacques-Cartier ☎ 514/875-6134 🕔 Daily 10–6 🚇 Champ-de-Mars 🚌 38

GALERIE ELCA LONDON
www.elcalondon.com
This is currently the only gallery in the city exclusively devoted to Inuit arts and crafts; some of the prices for the gallery-quality art and artifacts are prohibitive, but it is worth coming anyway simply to admire what's on show.
⊞ G10 ✉ 224 rue Saint-Paul Ouest ☎ 514/282-1173

🕔 Tue–Sat 10–5 🚇 Place d'Armes

LA GUILDE GRAPHIQUE
www.guildegraphique.com
Come here for a wide array of prints, engravings and etchings from different eras and in various different styles and genres. An excellent place to browse for gifts to take home.
⊞ G11 ✉ 9 rue Saint-Paul Ouest ☎ 514/844-3438 🕔 Mon–Fri 10–6, Sat 10–7, Sun 12–5 🚇 Place d'Armes

MARCHÉ DU VIEUX
This is a great place to shop for gourmet foods, including a wide range of tasty treats from Québec's artisan food producers and farmers. You can often try before you buy, which makes it even harder to resist.
⊞ G10 ✉ 8 rue Saint-Paul Est ☎ 514/393-2772 🕔 Daily 7–7 (to 9pm in summer) 🚇 Champ-de-Mars

MORTIMER SNODGRASS
www.shop.mortimersnodgrass.com
The gift shop stocks an eccentric collection that includes cards, stationery, home decor, puzzles for all ages, quality toys, spa luxuries, and even gifts for pets. Definitely different, with some retro items, some quirky, most irresistible.
⊞ G11 ✉ 56 rue Notre

Dame Ouest ☎ 514/499-2851 ⓘ Mon–Thu 10–5, Fri 10–7, Sat 10–6 🚇 Place d'Armes

NOËL ETERNEL
www.noeleternel.com
It's always Christmas here, with a great variety of high-quality ornaments, decorations and collectible items from around the world—all designed for the festive season.
✚ F11 ✉ 461 rue Saint-Sulpice ☎ 514/285-4944 or 888/595-4944 ⓘ Jan–Apr Tue–Sat 10–5; May–Dec Mon–Wed 9–6, Thu–Sun 9–8 🚇 Place d'Armes

POINTE-À-CALLIÈRE
www.pacmuseum.qc.ca
Vieux-Montréal may be littered with second-rate souvenir stores, but for a superior memento of the city visit this museum gift shop in the Ancienne-Douane (Old Customs) building. It has an excel lent selection of books on art and local history and archaeology, pieces of First Nations art, craft items and reproduction artifacts from Québec and around the world.
✚ G11 ✉ 150 rue Saint-Paul Ouest ☎ 514/872-9150 ⓘ Tue–Sun 11–6 🚇 Place d'Armes

ROLAND DUBUC
www.rolanddubuc.com
The studio-boutique of jeweler Roland Dubuc is the only place you can buy his elegant, unique pieces, each sculpted

from a single piece of gold or silver. The complexity of the twists and folds in the metal is enthralling.
✚ F12 ✉ 163 rue Saint-Paul Ouest ☎ 514/844-1221 ⓘ Tue–Fri 11–6, Sat–Sun 11–5 🚇 Place d'Armes

ROONEY
www.rooneyshop.com
This is a trendy clothing store/art gallery, with works by internationally known artists on vast exposed-brick walls. Clothing lines include Ella Moss, Hudson, Rocksmith, Yumi Kim, Casette, Corpus and many more.
✚ F12 ✉ 395 rue Notre-Dame Ouest ☎ 514/543-6234 ⓘ Mon–Wed 11.30–6.30, Thu–Fri 11.30–8, Sat–Sun 12–5 🚇 Square Victoria

RUE SAINT-PAUL
This street is home to a wide variety of stores,

MUSICAL SOUVENIRS
For something tonier, consider music. Because of its linguistic isolation, Québec has produced a rich popular culture of its own that's better known in France than in the US or even the rest of Canada. Try Archambault (▷ 78) for the latest hits, or look for CDs by *chansonniers* Gilles Vigneault and Félix Leclerc or seminal rock musician Robert Charlebois.

but is especially worth visiting for its many art galleries and craft shops. Most sell work by local and other Québécois artists and craftspeople, in a wide variety of styles. Even if you don't intend to buy, the quality of the items on sale make it worth looking into the galleries.
✚ G10–11 ✉ Rue Saint-Paul 🚇 Champ-de-Mars

SALON DES MÉTIERS D'ART DU QUÉBEC
www.metiers-d-art.qc.ca/smaq/
This Marché Bonsecours outlet is a treasure house of wonderful craft, artisan and other design objects. The beautiful selection includes glass, ceramics, items crafted out of wood and jewelry, from the studios of 100 craftspeople based across the province.
✚ G10 ✉ 350 rue Saint-Paul Est ☎ 514/878-2787, Ext 1 ⓘ Mon–Sat 11–9, Sun 11–6 🚇 Champ-de-Mars

STEVE'S MUSIC STORE
www.stevesmusic.com
This large and rambling store on the fringes of Vieux-Montréal is a magnet for musicians of every stripe, offering instruments, sheet music, songbooks and musical accessories.
✚ F11 ✉ 51 Saint-Antoine Ouest ☎ 514/878-2216 ⓘ Mon–Wed 9–6, Thu–Fri 9–9, Sat 9–5, Sun 12–5 🚇 Place d'Armes

VIEUX-MONTRÉAL SHOPPING

Entertainment and Nightlife

BATEAU MOUCHE DINNER CRUISE

www.bateaumouche.com
Cruise with fabulous views of the river and the city and dine on a five- or six-course gourmet feast, accompanied by live music—usually either cool jazz or romantic waltzes.
➕ G11 ✉ Quai Jacques-Cartier ☎ 514/849-9952 or 800/361-9952 🕐 Mid-May to mid-Oct daily, departing at 7pm; duration 3.5 hours
🖐 Expensive 🚇 Champ-de-Mars

LE CABARET DU ROY

www.oyez.ca
This restaurant and cabaret won't be to all tastes, as the music, costume, food and comedy all have an historic "New France" theme. You're served by "characters" from the Middle Ages. Most of the week it is open only to booked groups of 25 or more, but it opens to all Friday to Sunday.
➕ G10 ✉ 363 rue de la Commune Est ☎ 514/907-9000 🕐 Fri–Sat from 5.30pm. Terrace daily 11.30–10
🚇 Champ-de-Mars

CENTAUR THEATRE

www.centaurtheatre.com
The city's foremost English-language theater has a grand setting in the city's former Stock Exchange Building.
➕ F11 ✉ 453 rue Saint-François-Xavier
☎ 514/288-3161
🚇 Place d'Armes

LES 2 PIERROTS

www.2pierrots.com
A crowded and convivial venue devoted to Québécois folk music. Performances are on the terrace in fine weather.
➕ G11 ✉ 104 rue Saint-Paul Est ☎ 514/861-1270
🕐 Fri–Sat from 8.30pm
🚇 Place d'Armes

IMAX

www.centredessciencesde
montreal.com
If you like big-screen movies, this is the place, in the same building as the Centre des Sciences.
➕ G11 ✉ Quai King-Edward ☎ 514/496-4724 or 877/496-4724 🕐 Daily from 10am; last screening begins 8pm 🚇 Place d'Armes

MODAVIE

www.modavie.com
The restaurant here is good for Mediterranean dishes and other standards, but most people come for the large central bar, and for the live jazz, for which there is no cover charge. There's a good choice of malts and cigars, and bar snacks are free during happy hour on weekdays.
➕ G11 ✉ 1 rue Saint-Paul Ouest ☎ 514/287-9582
🕐 Daily 11.30–10.30; jazz Sun–Wed 8–10pm, Thu–Sat 7–11pm 🚇 Place d'Armes

PUB ST-PAUL

www.pubstpaul.com
The chief charms of this airy and friendly pub, with its rustic brick walls, flagstone floors and wooden beams, are its position close to the river and the views. On one of the area's delightful cobbled streets, it offers reasonable food, a wide range of beers and live music Friday and Saturday night.
➕ G11 ✉ 124 rue Saint-Paul Est ☎ 514/874-0485
🕐 Daily 11am–3am
🚇 Champ-de-Mars

VELVET

An intimate and fun club a block back from the waterfront with plenty of inviting dark corners. The music is mostly electro with the odd serving of pop and disco.
➕ G10 ✉ 420 rue Saint-Gabriel ☎ 514/878-9782
🕐 Tue–Sun 10pm–3am
🚇 Place d'Armes

CIRQUE DU SOLEIL

This circus has come a long way since it was founded on the quays of Montréal's Old Port waterfront in 1984. Its dance, acrobatics, costumes and drama has made it an international success. It has resident companies in Las Vegas and elsewhere, and its international headquarters in Montréal, where new recruits train. Performances are staged in the blue-and-yellow tents on the Vieux-Port quayside (☎ 514/790–1245; www.cirquedusoleil.com).

Restaurants

PRICES

Prices are approximate, based on a 3-course meal for one person.

$$$	over $40
$$	$20–$40
$	under $20

AUBERGE LE SAINT-GABRIEL ($$$)

www.aubergesaint-gabriel.com
This characterful inn was founded in 1754 and is said to be the oldest in North America. The dining rooms are large, with seating on the terrace, and the setting is suitably venerable, with a lovely fireplace and French and Québécois cooking.
🚺 G11 ✉ Rue Saint-Gabriel ☎ 514/878-3561 🕐 Apr–Aug daily lunch and dinner; Sep–Mar Tue–Fri lunch and dinner, Sat dinner 🚇 Place d'Armes

BONAPARTE ($$$)

www.restaurantbonaparte.com
Sit in the fireplace room overlooking rue Saint-Sacrement and you'll swear you're in Paris. The food is French, too.
🚺 F11 ✉ 443 rue Saint-François-Xavier ☎ 514/844 4368 🕐 Mon–Fri lunch and dinner, Sat–Sun dinner 🚇 Place d'Armes

BORIS BISTRO ($$)

www.borisbistro.com
French bistro food—such as homemade sausage or braised rabbit—served on a delightful tree-shaded terrace.
🚺 F12 ✉ 443 rue McGill ☎ 514/848-9575 🕐 May–Sep daily lunch, dinner; Oct–Apr Mon lunch, Tue–Fri lunch and dinner, Sat dinner 🚇 Square-Victoria

LE BOURLINGUEUR ($$)

www.lebourlingueur.ca
Fish and seafood are the main here, though non-seafood options are available. Try the specialty, poached salmon.
🚺 F11 ✉ 363 rue Saint-François-Xavier ☎ 514/845-3646 🕐 Daily lunch, dinner; closed Sat lunch Nov–Mar 🚇 Place d'Armes

CAFÉ STASH ($$)

www.stashcafe.com
Here you sit on pews to consume robust and warming Polish dishes—hot *borscht*, *pierogi* and several kinds of sausage.
🚺 G11 ✉ 200 rue Saint-Paul Ouest ☎ 514/845-6611 🕐 Daily lunch, dinner 🚇 Place d'Armes

ETHNIC FLAVORS

While it is French cuisine that dominates Montréal's dining scene, more than 30 ethnic groups are represented. Greek and Italian restaurants are enduringly popular in the city and Cantonese cooking has been a presence since the late 1800s. Refugees from Indochina in the 1970s opened Vietnamese restaurants and noodle shops. The current craze is for Thai food.

CHEZ L'ÉPICIER ($$$)

www.chezlepicier.com
Fresh market cuisine served in the surroundings of an old grocery store offers unusual variations on French dishes. Try the sweetbreads braised in apple juice and fresh thyme, or the salmon stew with salsify.
🚺 G10 ✉ 311 rue Saint-Paul ☎ 514/878-2232 🕐 Mon–Fri lunch and dinner, Sat–Sun dinner 🚇 Champ-de-Mars

CLUB CHASSE ET PECHE ($$)

www.leclubchasseetpeche.com
With just a coat of arms announcing its presence, this secretive little place is well worth seeking out for the deliciously imaginative food. Try braised piglet risotto with foie gras shavings, or venison with physalis purée, cashews and chocolate.
🚺 G11 ✉ 423 rue St-Claude ☎ 514/861-1112 🕐 Tue–Sat dinner 🚇 Champ-de-Mars, Place d'Armes

LA CONCESSION ($)

www.la-concession.com
This chic café in Vieux-Montréal serves chocolates, pastries and first-class sandwiches, as well as hot lunches. The fixed-price menus are good value. In summer sample the rich ice creams.
🚺 F11 ✉ 75 rue Notre-Dame Ouest ☎ 514/844-8750 🕐 Mon–Fri 7–7, Sat–Sun 9–5 🚇 Place d'Armes

VIEUX-MONTRÉAL RESTAURANTS

DA EMMA ($$)

Stone-walled basement room near the Vieux-Port. The cuisine is Italian; try fettucine with porcini mushrooms or tender roast baby pig.

⊞ G12 ✉ 777 rue de la Commune Ouest ☎ 514/392-1568 ⏱ Mon–Fri lunch, dinner, Sat dinner 🚇 Square-Victoria

GANDHI ($)

www.restaurantgandhi.com
Alternatives to French and Italian cuisine are rare in the Vieux-Port area, so this modern Indian restaurant, with crisp white napery and smart wood floors, makes a pleasant change. None of the food is too heavily spiced, and there are plenty of good vegetarian options.

⊞ G11 ✉ 230 rue Saint-Paul Ouest ☎ 514/845-5866 ⏱ Mon–Fri lunch, dinner, Sat–Sun dinner 🚇 Place d'Armes

GRAZIELLA ($$–$$$)

www.restaurantgraziella.ca
Simple northern-Italian dishes with a flair for presentation and taste. A first course of feather-light ricotta gnocchi sets the stage without dulling your appetite for hearty mains.

⊞ F12 ✉ 116 rue McGill ☎ 514/876-0116 ⏱ Mon–Fri lunch, dinner, Sat dinner 🚇 Square-Victoria

THE HAMBAR ($$$)

www.hotelstpaul.com
Super-trendy restaurant in the boutique Hôtel Saint-Paul serves bold, market cuisine to a fashionable crowd. Excellent wine list.

⊞ F12 ✉ 355 rue McGill ☎ 514/876-2823 ⏱ Daily lunch and dinner 🚇 Square-Victoria

LE LOCAL ($$$)

www.resto-lelocal.com
In the large dining room or on the terrace during the summer, Montréal's young and hip feast on decadent dishes including salmon tartar with truffle oil and lime, or roasted scallops with pea purée.

⊞ F12 ✉ 740 rue William ☎ 514/397-7737 ⏱ Mon–Fri 11.30am–midnight, Sat 5.30–midnight, Sun 5.30–11.30 🚇 Place d'Armes

OLIVE ET GOURMANDO ($)

www.oliveetgourmando.com
A superb bakery that offers salads, panini and delicious hot or cold sandwiches with generous, often exotic, fillings.

POPULAR MESS

Québec's own contribution to fast-food culture is something called *poutine* (literally "mess"). It consists of a huge plate of French fries, covered liberally with lumps of pale yellow cheese curds and drowned in thick, brown gravy. Another fast-food favorite is barbecued chicken—a crispy-skin, spit-roasted bird served in a spicy sauce.

⊞ G11 ✉ 315 rue Saint-Paul Ouest ☎ 514/350-1083 ⏱ Tue–Sat 8–6

SCENA ($$)

www.scena.ca
Scena is one of several places to eat on the Vieux-Port waterfront, and stands out by virtue of its big open-air terraces from which you can watch the world go by or soak up the sun. Food has a contemporary French bistro flavor.

⊞ G11 ✉ Quai Jacques-Carterin ☎ 514/288-0914 ⏱ Sun–Thu 11.30–10, Fri–Sat 11.30–midnight 🚇 Place d'Armes

TATAMI ($$)

This is an ideal place to stop on a tour of Vieux-Montréal. Grilled, spicy beef, salmon, chicken and squid are served in lacquered boxes along with salad and sticky rice.

⊞ F11 ✉ 140 rue Notre-Dame Ouest ☎ 514/845-5864 ⏱ Mon–Sat lunch, dinner 🚇 Place d'Armes

TOQUE! ($$$)

www.restaurant-toque.com
Toque! has been one of Montréal's gastronomic temples for years, and its contemporary French and Asian fusion food has lost nothing over the time. First choice for a treat.

⊞ F11 ✉ 900 place Jean-Paul-Riopelle, near rue Saint-François-Xavier ☎ 514/499-2084 ⏱ Tue–Fri lunch and dinner, Sat dinner 🚇 Place d'Armes

Downtown

Lovely churches, venerable museums and peaceful squares sit beside glittering skyscrapers, dramatic art galleries and busy shopping streets, while beneath is another world entirely, the Underground City.

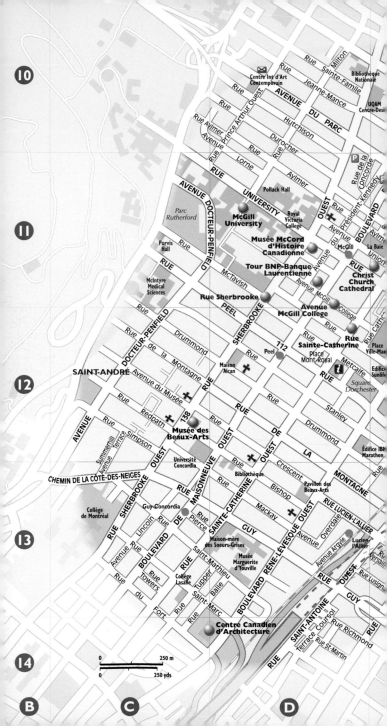

10

11

12

13

14

Rue Milton
Rue Sainte-Famille
Bibliothèque Nationale
Centre Int. d'Art Contemporain
Rue Jeanne-Mance
UQAM Centre-Desi
AVENUE DU PARC
Rue
Rue Prince Arthur Ouest
Rue Aylmer
Hutchison
Durocher
Avenue
Rue
Lorne
Aylmer
RUE UNIVERSITY
RUE DOCTEUR-PENFIELD
AVENUE
P Rue de la Concorde
Rue
OUEST
Pollack Hall
Président-Kennedy
BOULEVARD
Parc Rutherford
McGill University
Royal Victoria College
Avenue
Aylme
Musée McCord d'Histoire Canadienne
McGill
La Baie
Purvis Hall
Rue
Tour BNP-Banque Laurentienne
Union
RUE
Christ Church Cathedral
McIntyre Medical Sciences
Mctavish
RUE
Rue Cath
Rue Sherbrooke
SHERBROOKE
Avenue McGill
Avenue McGill College
RUE
PEEL
Rue
College
Place Ville-Ma
DOCTEUR-PENFIELD
Drummond
Rue
112
Rue Sainte-Catherine
Rue
Peel
Place Mont-Royal
Metcalfe
Rue
RUE
Édifice Sunlif
SAINT-ANDRÉ
Rue de la Montagne
Maison Alcan
RUE
i
Square Dorchester
Avenue du Musée
RUE
Rue
AVENUE
Rue Redpath
Simpson
738
Rue
OUEST
Stanley
Musée des Beaux-Arts
DE
Drummond
Summerhill
Avenue Terrace
RUE DOCTEUR-PENFIELD
OUEST
Crescent
LA
Édifice IBM Marathon
Université Concordia
Rue
MONTAGNE
CHEMIN DE LA CÔTE-DES-NEIGES
MAISONNEUVE
Rue
Bibliothèque
Bishop
Pavillon des Beaux-Arts
RUE LUCIEN-L'ALLIER
Collège de Montréal
RUE SHERBROOKE
Guy-Concordia
SAINTE-CATHERINE
Mackay
Avenue
Overdale
Lucien-L'Allier
RUE
Rue
DE
Rue Pierce
GUY
Avenue Argyle
Rue Versailli
Lincoln
Rue
BOULEVARD
Saint-Mathieu
Maison-mère des Soeurs-Grises
BOULEVARD RENÉ-LÉVESQUE OUEST
Rue Lusign
Avenue Rue
Rue
Musée Marguerite d'Youville
OUEST
GUY
Collège Lasalle
Tupper
RUE
Rue Towers
Baile
RUE SAINT-ANTOINE
Rue Richmond
du
Saint-Marc
Centre Canadien d'Architecture
Terrace
Rue Courtol
Rue St-Martin
Fort
RUE

0   250 m
0   250 yds

B   **C**   **D**

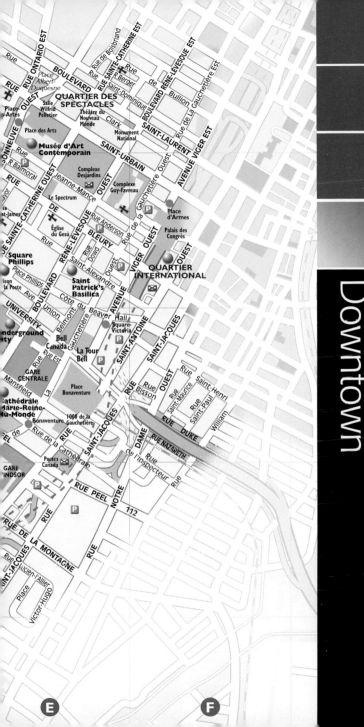

Cathédrale Marie-Reine-du-Monde

The huge copper cupola (right) and intricate statues atop the Cathédrale (left)

THE BASICS

www.cathedrale
catholiquedemontreal.org

➕ E12

✉ 1085 rue de la Cathédrale

☎ 514/866-1661

🕐 Mon–Fri 7–6.15, Sat–Sun 7.30–6.15. Closed during services

🚇 Bonaventure

🚌 107, 150, 410, 420, 535

♿ Very good, but a steep ramp

🎟 Free

HIGHLIGHTS

● Stained glass
● High altar
● Bourget Chapel

Mary Queen of the World Cathedral brings a taste of the Italian Renaissance into the heart of Montréal. Dwarfed now by skyscrapers, the cathedral was a daring monument to 19th-century Roman Catholic triumphalism.

St. Peter's in miniature Bishop Ignace Bourget, who began the cathedral three years after Canadian confederation, intended to underline papal supremacy and show that Catholicism still dominated what was then the largest city in the Dominion. So he set the cathedral, a one-quarter-size replica of St. Peter's in Rome, at the heart of the city's Anglo-Protestant district. Begun in 1870, the building was completed in 1894.

Step inside In contrast to the lovely intimacy of Notre-Dame in Vieux-Montréal, the interior is somber, although the interiors of both churches are the work of architect Victor Bourgeau. The gloom was intended to intensify the effect of candles and accentuate the rose windows. The opulent high altar features a copy of the vast *baldacchino*, or altar canopy, by Bernini in St. Peter's, while the first little chapel in the left aisle has a red-flocked sanctuary filled with medals and saintly relics. Bishop Bourget is interred in a second chapel on the same side of the church, his recumbent figure surrounded by the tombs of his successors. On a pillar facing the bishop's tomb is a memorial to the men from the diocese who served in the Papal Zouaves in the fight against Italian nationalists.

One of the world's most impressive architectural museums, in a superb space

Centre Canadien d'Architecture

There's something fitting about the layout of what is arguably the world's premier architectural museum. Its U-plan fortress embraces an impressive 19th-century mansion.

Temple of architecture The gray limestone facade is long, low and virtually windowless, and the front door, at the building's western end, appears an afterthought. But that door leads into six beautifully lit halls given over to changing exhibits ranging from the academic to the whimsical—displays on modernist theory and American lawn culture are equally at home. Incorporated into the complex is the 1877 Shaughnessy Mansion, with its art nouveau conservatory, built for Canadian Pacific Railway chairman Sir Thomas Shaughnessy. Across the street, in an island of green between two busy main thoroughfares, is a garden designed by Melvin Charney, where fanciful fragments tell the story of architecture.

Phyllis Lambert The woman behind all this is architect Phyllis Lambert, a defender of Montréal's architectural heritage, who founded the center in 1979 and presided, with architect Peter Rose, over the building of its present home (1985–89). She also contributed her own impressive collection, now expanded to 100,000 prints and drawings (some by Leonardo da Vinci and Michelangelo), 55,000 architectural photographs and 200,000 books and publications dating from 15th-century manuscripts to the present. The archives are open by appointment.

THE BASICS

www.cca.qc.ca
🔢 D14
✉ 1920 rue Baile, between rues Saint-Marc and du Fort
☎ 514/939-7000
🕐 Wed, Fri 11–6, Sat–Sun 11–5, Thu 11–9
Ⓜ Guy-Concordia (St. Mathieu exit)
🚌 15, 150
♿ Excellent
💵 Moderate (free with a weekly or monthly transit pass)
❓ Excellent bookstore

HIGHLIGHTS

- Facade
- Halls
- Mansion
- Conservatory
- Gardens

DOWNTOWN TOP 25

Christ Church Cathedral

Inside the cathedral (left); a skyscraper towers over the spire (right)

THE BASICS

www.montrealcathedral.ca

🏠 E11

✉ 635 rue Sainte-Catherine Ouest and 1444 avenue Union

☎ Cathedral staff 514/843-6577

🕐 Daily 8–6. Closed during services

Ⓜ McGill

♿ Very good; ramps from street

💷 Free

❓ Midday and evening choral and organ concerts

HIGHLIGHTS

● Choral Evensong (4pm daily)
● Nave altar
● Carved angels in the Chapterhouse
● Coventry Cross
● Bishop's Throne
● Chapel of St. John
● Pulpit

The seat of Montréal's Anglican bishop is a graceful ship of serenity floating (almost literally) on a sea of commerce. There are department stores on either side of it, a skyscraper behind, and a shopping mall right underneath.

Copy This beautifully simple church is the city's Anglican cathedral, built between 1857 and 1859 at the instigation of Francis Fulford, Montréal's first Anglican bishop. Its neo-Gothic style is reminiscent of a 14th-century English church, but its plan is actually a straight copy of the Anglican cathedral in Fredericton, N. B., which was designed by the same architect, Frank Wills. The steeple had problems, proving to be too heavy for the soft, unstable ground, and was replaced in 1927 with one made of aluminum plates, doctored to match the stone of the rest of the church. Among the notable objects inside the church is a cross (left and above the pulpit) made from nails rescued from the bombed Coventry Cathedral in England.

Money matters Over time soaring towers have dwarfed the cathedral, while high maintenance costs and dwindling congregations led to a budgetary shortfall. The Anglican authorities found an imaginative solution in 1985 when they leased the land around and beneath the cathedral to developers. The church now sits atop Les Promenades Cathédrale (▷ 63), a busy mall. Shoppers, office workers and store clerks of all faiths retreat to the cathedral at midday for free concerts and organ recitals.

Musée d'Art Contemporain

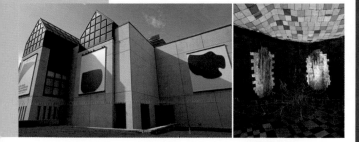

The building is contemporary (left), as are the works of art inside (right)

Montréal boasts one of Canada's most important museums of contemporary art. The stark, modern building is impressive, from its offbeat doors to the distinctive angular galleries and central atrium.

On the Move Founded in 1964 by the Québec government, the museum occupied three different buildings before moving into its present home, a superb plain-faced modern building only a stone's throw from Place des Arts, in 1992. It originally focused on the work of indigenous Québécois artists, but the museum has increasingly widened its scope and mounts temporary exhibitions by artists from around the world.

The paintings Works in the gallery date from around 1939 up to the present, with at least 60 percent of the more than 5,000 works of art in the museum's collection by Québécois artists. Among those represented are David Moore, Alfred Pellan and Jean-Paul Riopelle, and there are 75 paintings by Montréal artist Paul-Émile Borduas. Other Canadian artists include Jack Bush, Michael Snow and Barbara Steinman. Works by Picasso, Lichtenstein and Warhol are also on display. There is a growing video art collection. Much of the permanent collection is often moved out to make way for temporary exhibitions, such as the hyperrealist portraits of Winnipeg artist Karel Funk, photographic creations by Brazilian Vik Muniz, the Thomas Hirschhorn installations *Jumbo Spoons* and *Big Cake*, and exhibitions of new acquisitions. Remember to look round the sculpture garden.

THE BASICS

www.macm.org

E10

185 rue Sainte-Catherine Ouest at rue Jeanne-Mance

514/847-6226

Tue, Thu–Sun 11–6, Wed 11–9

Le Contemporain restaurant (lunch Tue–Wed, lunch and dinner Thu–Fri, dinner Sat)

Place-des-Arts

15, 55, 80, 129, 535

Very good

Expensive; free Wed from 5pm for collection; reduced rate for exhibitions

Guided tours, live music events and children's activities

HIGHLIGHTS

● Architecture
● *Lips*, Geneviève Cadieux
● Steel atrium
● Sculpture garden
● *L'Île fortifiée*, Paul-Émile Borduas

McGill University

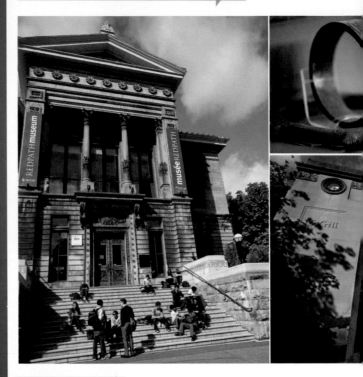

HIGHLIGHTS

● Roddick Gates
● Green space
● Redpath Museum
● Views
● Arts Building

TIPS

● Energetic visitors can rent bicycles, skates, snowshoes, Nordic skis and kick-sleds, inner tubes and pedal boats.
● The grassy slope above Beaver lake is dotted with interesting sculptures left over from a 1964 exhibition.

Diverse and attractive architecture defines this fine university on the lower slopes of Mont-Royal, along with one of Canada's oldest and most eclectic museums. It's a privileged place from which to view the city and feel its vibrant rhythms.

Urban country The university opened in 1821 on a patch of pasture donated for the purpose by fur trader and land speculator James McGill. Since then, Montréal has spread northwards and now surrounds the 32ha (80-acre) campus. A great deal of green space is preserved within the boundaries of the university, including the "lower field" in the mid-campus area, where students will be seen studying on the grass, playing sports or just chilling out on sunny days. The lawns near the Arts Building are also attractive, with fine old trees.

Clockwise from left: taking a break on the steps of Redpath Museum; an ornament from the Congo and an African sculpture; a view inside the museum; the Roddick Gates, at the university's main entrance

Architecture The Greek Revival Roddick Gates guard the main entrance to the university on rue Sherbrooke Ouest, and behind them a tree-lined avenue leads to the 1839 neoclassical domed Arts Building, the oldest building on campus, containing the Moyse Hall, a theater. Along the avenue's east side are two further fine neoclassical buildings designed by Sir Andrew Taylor in the 1890s; Taylor also designed the Library, with its elaborate carvings. Percy Nobbs's 1908 Macdonald Engineering Building is in the English Baroque Revival style. But the most beautiful structure on campus is the templelike Redpath Museum of Natural History. The museum houses a huge and wonderfully whimsical collection that includes dinosaur bones, old coins, African art and a shrunken head. Under the trees a bronze James McGill hurries across campus.

THE BASICS

www.mcgill.ca
➕ D11
✉ 859 rue Sherbrooke Ouest
📞 Welcome Centre 514/398-6555; Redpath Museum 514/398-4086, ext 00549
🕐 Welcome Centre Mon–Fri 9–4; Redpath Museum Mon–Fri 9–5, Sun 11–5
🚇 McGill
♿ Fair
💲 Free

Musée des Beaux-Arts

A painting, Mah-Min (1848), by Paul Kane (left) displayed in the museum (right)

THE BASICS

www.mbam.qc.ca

🕂 C12

✉ 1379–1380 rue Sherbrooke Ouest

☎ 514/285-2000

🕐 Tue–Fri 11–5, Sat–Sun 10–5, some exhibitions also Wed 5–9

🍴 Café des Beaux-Arts; also cafeteria

Ⓖ Guy-Concordia

🚌 24

♿ Good

✋ Free permanent exhibition. Special shows expensive (half-price Wed 5–9)

HIGHLIGHTS

● *Portrait of a Young Woman*, Rembrandt
● *Portrait of a Man*, El Greco
● *Torso*, Henry Moore
● *October*, James Tissot
● *Automatic paintings*

Canada's oldest art museum (founded in 1860) consists of two fine buildings facing each other across rue Sherbrooke Ouest, housing the country's best collection of Canadian paintings, as well as First Nations artifacts, and old masters.

A fine museum This venerable institution is one of North America's finest galleries. Completed in 1912 and enlarged in 1976, the main building is unmistakable, with its stolid Vermont marble front and four large Ionic columns. Across the street stands the Desmarais Pavilion (1991), a stunning modern building designed by Montréal architect Moshe Safdie.

The collection Canadian paintings range from works imported by the French settlers through to those by the Toronto-based Group of Seven. There are also period furnishings, drawings, engravings, silverware and art from ancient China, Japan, Egypt, Greece and South America. Among the old masters are works by Rembrandt and El Greco; Picasso, Henry Moore and Impressionists represent more recent eras.

Further expansion Constantly growing, the collections have been further expanded by the entire contents of the former Musée Marc-Aurèle Fortin and by Mrs Liliane M. Stewart's collection of some 900 American industrial-design exhibits. An exciting project has been unveiled to convert the Erskine and American Church next door to house the collections of Canadian art.

A totem pole (left) and a sculpture by Dave McGary (2005; right) in the museum (middle)

Musée McCord d'Histoire Canadienne

The McCord Museum of Canadian History possesses a huge range of objects, including Native Canadian culture and an important photographic collection, offering an insight into Montréal's past.

Bigger and bigger Montréal lawyer David Ross McCord (1844–1930) was a collector with an insatiable appetite for anything connected with Canadian history. In the 1920s he gave his huge collection of books, furniture, clothing, guns, paintings, documents, toys and photographs to McGill University, where it was housed in the McGill Union Building (1906). The museum continues McCord's desire to present history to the nation. A $20-million renovation in 1992 doubled the museum's size, but still there is space to display only a fraction of the 1,375,000 items.

Photographic collection The museum is strongest on the culture and history of Native Canadians, and includes some 16,600 costumes. Also remarkable are the Notman Photographic Archives, a collection of prints produced by photographic pioneer William Notman, who captured Victorian life in Montréal. The photographs include balls, soldiers marching and members of the exclusive Montréal Athletic Association in snowshoes. Each of the hundreds of people shown in these pictures was photographed individually in the studio and then the photos were mounted onto an appropriate background. In all there are 450,000 photographs in the Archives, plus 800,000 images taken by other photographers.

THE BASICS

www.mccord-museum.qc.ca

⊞ D11

✉ 690 rue Sherbrooke Ouest at rue Victoria

☎ 514/398-7100

🕐 Tue–Fri 10–6, Sat–Sun 10–5, Wed also 5–9

🍴 The McCord Café

Ⓜ McGill

🚌 24, 125

♿ Good

💰 Expensive (free Wed 5–9)

❓ Guided tours, reading room

HIGHLIGHTS

● Notman Photographic Archives
● First Nations collection
● Historic prints and maps
● Decorative arts collection

Saint Patrick's Basilica

TOP
25

Stained-glass window (left); two apostles on the pulpit (middle); the lofty interior (right)

THE BASICS

www.stpatricksmtl.ca

🕂 E11

✉ 454 boulevard René-Lévesque Ouest

☎ 514/866-7379

🕐 Daily 9–6

🚇 Square-Victoria or McGill

♿ Fair

💲 Free

HIGHLIGHTS

● Pulpit
● Sanctuary lamp
● Darcy McGee's pew

TIPS

● Take a break in the pleasant garden space on the west side of the basilica.
● Hear the Saint Patrick's Basilica choir during the celebration of the Eucharist on Sunday at 11am September to June, in Latin every third Sunday of the month.

Built for Montréal's Irish Catholics, this graceful neo-Gothic building has a beautiful interior, with delicate mosaics and stained-glass windows that glow in the afternoon sunlight.

Our church Bishop Ignace Bourget gave only grudging approval when the Irish Catholics asked for a church of their own in 1843. The Mass, he reasoned, was in Latin, and most of the Irish spoke Gaelic at home so the Frenchness of the existing churches was immaterial. He saw no reason why they could not go to church with their French-speaking brethren. But the Irish community, who had mostly come to escape famine in their homeland, were adamant that they wanted their own place of worship, and with help from the Sulpician priests they erected a graceful neo-Gothic church.

Then there was light When the sun floods through the stained-glass figures of the four Evangelists it fills the soaring nave with a honey-color glow. The vault over the sanctuary gleams with green and gold mosaics and the air smells of beeswax and incense. The pulpit and huge sanctuary lamp are highly decorated, painted panels line the walls of the nave, and statues of bishops, martyrs, princesses and peasants jostle for space on the main altar and the niches of the side altars. Thomas Darcy McGee, one of the fathers of the confederation, was buried in Saint Patrick's after his assassination in 1868. His pew is marked with a Canadian flag.

Shopping in Montréal's
"Underground City" (left
and right); 1000 de la
Gauchetière (middle)

TOP
25

Underground City

Harsh winters pale into insignificance
in Montréal because of this vast Underground City. There are plenty of shops
and restaurants, and easy access to those
above ground, plus transportation links.

Beginnings Montréal's vast Underground
City (officially known as RÉSO, from Réseau
Piétonnier Souterrain) began in the early 1960s,
when a mall full of shops and boutiques opened
underneath the main plaza of place Ville-Marie,
the city's first modern skyscraper. Both it and the
neighboring Queen Elizabeth Hotel were built
over the Canadian National Railway's tracks so
it seemed natural enough to link both of them
with Central Station, and to place Bonaventure to
the south. The idea caught on and really took off
when the Métro opened in 1966.

Growth The underground now has more than
32km (20 miles) of wide, well-lit tunnels, mostly
clustered around 10 of the Métro system's 68
stations. The system encompasses eight major
hotels, two universities, both train stations, more
than 1,700 boutiques, two department stores,
more than 200 restaurants, at least 40 theaters
and other entertainment venues, and the Centre
Bell, but the only church with its own link to
the system is Christ Church Cathedral. Bear in
mind before venturing below ground that it's not
always easy to navigate, so get a map and be
prepared to ask the way. Remember that though
some are underground, most of the shops and
malls are above ground.

THE BASICS

✚ E12
✉ Access at Métro
stations in center
🕐 Sun–Fri 5.30am–
12.30am, Sat 5.30am–1am
🚇 Peel, McGill,
Bonaventure,
Place-des-Arts,
Square-Victoria
♿ Fair

HIGHLIGHTS

● Place Ville-Marie
● Les Halles de la Gare
● 1000 de la Gauchetière
and ice rink
● Atrium of the ICAD
Building
● Centre CPD Capital and
Terrasse du Parquet

More to See

AVENUE MCGILL COLLEGE

This short wide boulevard runs from Cathcart near Place Ville-Marie up to McGill University's Roddick Gates. If you stand on the Place Ville-Marie plaza, you get a beautiful sweeping view of the mountains and the campus framed by glass office towers. This is a great place to eat lunch outdoors in summer.
➕ D11 🚇 McGill

QUARTIER INTERNATIONAL

www.qimtl.qc.ca

Between downtown and Vieux-Montréal, this area has been redeveloped over the last decade. The Palais de Congrès (Convention Centre) is here, and towering office blocks represent the finest of contemporary architecture, but the Quartier International is also people-friendly. A Cultural Discovery Walk incorporates all the highlights, including around 20 office buildings with art from Montréal museums on display. Place Jean-Paul Riopelle, opposite the north side of the

Palais de Congrès, is named after the artist and contains his magnificent fountain sculpture, encircled by a ring of fire on summer evenings. Farther east, Square Victoria is a leafy area with lawns and benches, water jets, a monument to Queen Victoria, and the only Hector Guimard Métro entrance outside Paris (on permanent loan from the French capital).
➕ F11 ☎ 514/841-7766 🚇 Place d'Armes, Square-Victoria

RUE SAINTE-CATHERINE

Montréal's premier shopping street, rue Sainte-Catherine is also the longest commercial street in North America. Those with the stamina to walk its length would find character changes along the way, as it passes through the Quartier Latin, the Gay Village (▷ 94) and Quartier des Spectacles. In some places it is classy and upscale. Elsewhere it is a honeypot of mainstream shopping, with all the usual high-street favorites. Between May

The Secret Bench *on avenue McGill College*

and September many parts of the street are pedestrian-only and provide the stage for a wide variety of festivals and events through the year, not least Le Festival International de Montréal en Arts (www.festivaldesarts.org), when "BoulevArt" turns a long section of the street into eastern Canada's largest outdoor art gallery.
➕ D12 Ⓜ Peel, McGill

RUE SHERBROOKE

This grand thoroughfare cuts across Montréal island and is 31km (19 miles) long, but the section in this area includes the classiest shopping. The street's most interesting section flanks the area known as the Golden Square Mile (Atwater to Bleury), Montréal's most opulent district in the late 19th century. Although shops still line the street, it is no longer the exclusive domain of the luxury retailers that once catered to the district's wealthy mansion owners.
➕ D11 Ⓜ Peel, McGill

SQUARE PHILLIPS

An immense, pigeon-splattered statue of King Edward VII, sculpted by Philippe Hébert in 1914, dominates this pleasant open space on rue Sainte-Catherine, named after building contractor Thomas Phillips. In summer street vendors' stands compete with the square's shops. Christ Church Cathedral (▷ 50) is nearby.
➕ E11 Ⓜ McGill

TOUR BNP-BANQUE LAURENTIENNE

These twin blue-glass towers are eye-catching on the downtown skyline, dominating a particularly pleasant stretch of avenue McGill. The sculptural group *The Illuminated Crowd*, in front of the towers, represents Montréal's immigrant population. Raymond Mason's larger-than-life white figures create a stunning contrast to the towers' blue-tinted glass.
➕ D11 ✉ 1981 avenue McGill College Ⓜ McGill

Shops on rue Sainte-Catherine
Sculpture outside Tour BNP

Heart of Downtown

At street level this walk explores the dazzling high-rise heart of the modern city above the underground in the Cité Souterrain.

DISTANCE: 3km (2 miles) **ALLOW:** 1.5 hours

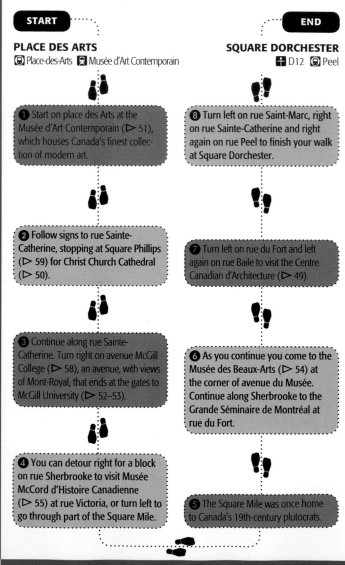

START

PLACE DES ARTS
🚇 Place-des-Arts 🏛 Musée d'Art Contemporain

END

SQUARE DORCHESTER
🚻 D12 🚇 Peel

❶ Start on place des Arts at the Musée d'Art Contemporain (▷ 51), which houses Canada's finest collection of modern art.

❽ Turn left on rue Saint-Marc, right on rue Sainte-Catherine and right again on rue Peel to finish your walk at Square Dorchester.

❷ Follow signs to rue Sainte-Catherine, stopping at Square Phillips (▷ 59) for Christ Church Cathedral (▷ 50).

❼ Turn left on rue du Fort and left again on rue Baile to visit the Centre Canadien d'Architecture (▷ 49).

❸ Continue along rue Sainte-Catherine. Turn right on avenue McGill College (▷ 58), an avenue, with views of Mont-Royal, that ends at the gates to McGill University (▷ 52–53).

❻ As you continue you come to the Musée des Beaux-Arts (▷ 54) at the corner of avenue du Musée. Continue along Sherbrooke to the Grande Séminaire de Montréal at rue du Fort.

❹ You can detour right for a block on rue Sherbrooke to visit Musée McCord d'Histoire Canadienne (▷ 55) at rue Victoria, or turn left to go through part of the Square Mile.

❺ The Square Mile was once home to Canada's 19th-century plutocrats.

Shopping

LA BAIE (THE BAY)
www.thebay.com
The Hudson's Bay Company, founded in 1891, still sells the company's distinctive blankets, as well as the full range of usual department store goods.
🔝 E11 ✉ 585 rue Sainte-Catherine Ouest at Square Phillips ☎ 514/281-4422 🕐 Sun–Wed 10–7, Thu–Fri 10–9, Sat 9–7 🚇 McGill

BIRKS
www.birks.com
One of the country's most prestigious and longest-established jewelers, particularly known for its fine silverware and classy blue packaging. You'll also find high-quality china and crystal. The store is particularly worth a visit for a look at its wonderfully striking art deco interior.
🔝 E11 ✉ 1240 Square Phillips ☎ 514/397-2511 🕐 Mon–Wed 10–6, Thu, Fri 10–9, Sat 9.30–5, Sun 12–5 🚇 McGill

LE CENTRE EATON
www.centreeatondemontreal.com
Ironically, the venerable Canadian department store that gave this mall its name closed its doors in 1999. But the mall's five floors of boutiques and shops are still thriving.
🔝 E12 ✉ 705 rue Sainte-Catherine Ouest ☎ 514/288-3708 🕐 Mon–Fri 10–9, Sat 10–7, Sun 11–6 🚇 McGill

COMPLEXE DESJARDINS
www.complexedesjardins.com
This vast multitiered complex is the largest mall in downtown. In addition to about 100 shops you'll find bistros, restaurants, cinemas, offices and a large piazza used for cultural events. Fountains and exotic plants make the place very pleasant.
🔝 E10 ✉ 150 rue Sainte-Catherine Ouest at Saint-Urbain ☎ 514/281-1870 🕐 Mon–Wed 9.30–6, Thu–Fri 9.30–9, Sat 9.30–5, Sun 12–5 🚇 Place-des-Arts

ÉDIFICE BELGO
This building is essentially a mall for art galleries, showcasing established and upcoming artists. Some of the best include Troise Points and Optica Centre for Contemporary Art.

SHOPPING DISTRICTS
Montréal's best shopping is in the malls close to the McGill Métro station and along rue Sainte-Catherine. Cheaper shops abound in Vieux-Montréal. More bohemian stores can be found around boulevard Saint-Laurent (The Main). Bookshops, galleries and antiques shops are in nearby rue Saint-Denis, while still other interesting options are springing up around avenue du Mont-Royal and rue Saint-Viateur.

🔝 E11 ✉ 372 rue Sainte-Catherine Ouest ☎ Troise Points 514/866-8008; Optica 514/874–1666 🕐 Wed–Fri 12–6, Sat 12–5 🚇 Place-des-Arts, Place-d'Armes

GUILDE CANADIENNE DES MÉTIERS D'ART
www.canadianguildofcrafts.com
Canadian crafts such as blown glass, porcelain, pewter, tapestry and jewelry, plus a permanent exhibition of Inuit, First Peoples and other Canadian artifacts.
🔝 C12 ✉ 1460-B rue Sherbrooke Ouest ☎ 514/849-6091 🕐 Tue–Fri 10–6, Sat 10–5 🚇 Guy-Concordia

HENRI HENRI
www.henrihenri.ca
One of the finest men's hat shops on the continent stocks everything from handwoven Panamas to jaunty berets and even baseball caps.
🔝 F10 ✉ 189 rue Sainte-Catherine Est, corner of rue Hôtel-de-Ville ☎ 514/288-0109 or 888/388-0109 🕐 Mon–Fri 10–6, Sat–Sun 10–5 🚇 Saint-Laurent, Berri-UQAM

OGILVY
www.ogilvycanada.com
Burberry, Godiva, Crabtree & Evelyn and top names in men's and women's wear all have their own little shops within this classy department store, along with the top-floor designer shops. Be there at noon

when the piper parades the store.

🔲 D13 ✉ 1307 rue Sainte-Catherine Ouest ☎ 514/842-7711 🕐 Mon–Wed 10–6, Thu–Fri 10–9, Sat 9–5, Sun 12–5 🚇 Peel

PARAGRAPHE BOOK STORE

www.paragraphbooks.com
Popular with serious book lovers and students. Lectures and readings by leading Canadian authors.

🔲 D11 ✉ 2220 avenue McGill College ☎ 514/845-5811 🕐 Mon–Fri 8am–9pm, Sat–Sun 9–9 🚇 McGill

PETIT MUSÉE

www.petitmusee.com
Sensational antiques from around the world, at stratospheric prices. It's worth taking a look even if you don't intend to buy.

🔲 C12 ✉ 1494 rue Sherbrooke Ouest ☎ 514/937-6161 🕐 Tue–Fri 9.30–5.30, Sat 10–5; also by appointment 🚇 Guy-Concordia

PLACE VILLE-MARIE

www.placevillemarie.com
The first underground mall that started it all has 100-plus shops.

🔲 E12 ✉ 1 place Ville-Marie ☎ 514/861-9393 🕐 Mon–Wed 9.30–6, Thu, Fri 9.30–9, Sat 9.30–5, Sun 12–5 🚇 Bonaventure

LES PROMENADES CATHÉDRALE

www.promenadescathedrale.com
The five-layer vertical mall was created under Christ Church Cathedral, and includes 60 shops, boutiques, cafés and restaurants, all connected to the Underground City (▷ 56).

🔲 E11 ✉ 625 rue Sainte-Catherine Ouest ☎ 514/845-8230 🕐 Mon–Wed 10–6, Thu, Fri 10–9, Sat 10–5, Sun 11–5 🚇 McGill

ROOTS

www.roots.com
Roots is now a national institution, full of inexpensive and timeless clothes, shoes and home furnishings.

🔲 D12 ✉ 1025 rue Sainte-Catherine Ouest ☎ 514/845-7995 🕐 Mon 10–5, Tue–Thu 10–7, Fri–Sat 10–9, Sun 9–6 🚇 McGill, Peel

RUDSAK

www.rudsak.com
Sleek and trendy fashions, footwear and accessories

MALL SHOPPING

The advantage of shopping in Montréal's state-of-the-art malls is that it's an all-season endeavor. Most of them are linked into the Underground City's (▷ 57) extensive network of tunnels and Métro lines. Many of the city's major department stores are also connected to the system, and some of them have become mini-malls, opening shops within shops to showcase designers such as Jean-Claude Chacok, Guy Laroche and Cacherel.

for women and men.

🔲 D13 ✉ 1400 rue Sainte-Catherine Ouest ☎ 514/844-1014 🕐 Mon–Wed 10–6, Thu, Fri 10–9, Sat 10–5, Sun 12–5 🚇 Guy-Concordia

SIMONS

www.simons.ca
Where La Baie is mostly traditional, Simons is a youthful department store, with an emphasis on good clothes for men and women.

🔲 D12 ✉ 977 rue Sainte-Catherine Ouest ☎ 514/282-1840 🕐 Mon–Wed 10–6, Thu, Fri 10–9, Sat 9.30–5, Sun 11–5.30 🚇 Peel

ULYSSES LA LIBRAIRIE DU VOYAGE

www.ulyssesguides.com
Travel books in French and English, as well as maps and assorted travel-related artifacts.

🔲 D11 ✉ 560 avenue du Président-Kennedy, near avenue Union ☎ 514/843-7222 🕐 Mon–Wed 10.30–6, Fri 10.30–6.30, Sat 10.30–5, Sun 12–5 🚇 McGill

L'UOMO MONTRÉAL

www.luomo-montreal.com
Top-name European designer clothing, footwear and accessories for men, with European-style tailors and expert wardrobe coordinators on hand to advise. Alteration service and world-wide delivery.

🔲 D12 ✉ 1452 rue Peel ☎ 514/844-1008 or 877/844-1008 🕐 Mon–Wed 9–6, Thu–Fri 9–8, Sat 9–5 🚇 Peel

Entertainment and Nightlife

DOWNTOWN ENTERTAINMENT AND NIGHTLIFE

CAFÉ-BAR SAINT-SUPLICE

www.lesaintsuplice.ca

This is a favorite among Montréal's students and is busy just about any time of day or night; it also boasts a vast terrace and offers music and other events.

➕ E10 ✉ 1680 rue Saint-Denis ☎ 514/844-9458 🕐 Bar daily 3.30pm–3am; restaurant Thu–Sat from 5pm 🚇 Berri-UQAM

CENTRE BELL

www.centrebell.ca

The home of the Montréal Canadiens also hosts big-name rock concerts.

➕ E13 ✉ 1260 rue de la Gauchetière Ouest ☎ 514/790-1245 🚇 Lucien-l'Allier, Bonaventure

CINÉMA BANQUE SCOTIA MONTRÉAL

Downtown center with 15 theaters—two with IMAX screens—that show films in French and English.

➕ D12 ✉ 977 rue Sainte-Catherine Ouest ☎ 514/842-0549 🚇 McGill

CLUB LOUNGE KARINA'S

www.winniesbar.com

One of the biggest and slickest clubs on trendy rue Crescent. A mix of live and recorded Latin, jazz, R&B and hip hop.

➕ D12 ✉ 1455 rue Crescent ☎ 514/288-0616 🕐 Thu–Sat 10pm–3am 🚇 Guy-Concordia

COMEDY NEST

www.thecomedynest.com

Renowned comedy club hosting top-notch touring stand-up acts.

➕ C14 ✉ Montreal Forum, 3rd Floor, rue Saint-Catherine at Atwater ☎ 514/932-6378 🚇 Atwater

HOUSE OF JAZZ

www.houseofjazz.ca

A bar, a restaurant and one of the best venues in the city for live jazz and blues.

➕ D11 ✉ 2060 rue Aylmer near rue Sherbrooke ☎ 514/842-8656 🕐 Mon–Wed 11.30am–1am, Thu–Fri 11am–3am, Sat 6pm–3am, Sun 6pm–1am 🚇 McGill

PLACE DES ARTS

www.laplacedesarts.com

Montréal's showcase for the performing arts has five major performance spaces and houses the Orchestre Symphonique de Montréal, Orchestre Métropolitain de Montréal, Opéra de Montréal and the city's principal ballet troupe. Call after 4pm for deeply discounted tickets to that evening's performance. Plays and an informal Sunday-morning breakfast concert series are also held here.

➕ E10 ✉ 260 boulevard de Maisonneuve Ouest ☎ Information 514/285-4200, tickets 514/842-2112, toll-free 866/842-2112 🕐 Box office Mon–Sat 10–6 🚇 Place-des-Arts

PUB SIR WINSTON CHURCHILL

www.winniesbar.com

English-style pub, known as "Winnies," with a dance floor.

➕ D12 ✉ 1455–59 rue Crescent ☎ 514/288-3814 🕐 Daily 11.30am–3am 🚇 Peel, Guy-Concordia

PUB LE VIEUX DUBLIN

www.dublinpub.ca

A much-loved Irish pub. Live Celtic music nights.

➕ E12 ✉ 636 rue Cathcart ☎ 514/861-4448 🕐 Daily 11am–3am. Food served Mon–Sat 11.30–3, 5–9.30, Sun 4.30–8 🚇 McGill

SALSATHÈQUE

Popular downtown Latin club; live music in addition to house DJs.

➕ D12 ✉ 1220 rue Peel at rue Sainte-Catherine Ouest ☎ 514/875-0016 🕐 Wed–Sat 10pm–3am 🚇 Peel

---

TICKETS

In October 2007 Montréal at last got a central ticket office handling bookings for the diverse range of events and activities in the city. Called La Vitrine, it is located at the place des Arts and offers comprehensive information about what's on, advance ticket sales or last-minute cut-price bargains. Drop in to the bureau, give them a call, or go online (2 rue Sainte-Catherine Ouest, ☎ 514/285-4545; http://lavitrine.com).

Restaurants

PRICES

Prices are approximate, based on a 3-course meal for one person.

$$$	over $40
$$	$20–$40
$	under $20

ANDIAMO ($$$)

www.andiamo.ca
Pan-Mediterranean flavors at this hip restaurant include Catalonian, Provençal, Ligurian and Adriatic influences. Calamari are crusted in Parmesan and poppy seeds, sea bream is finished with olive tapenade, and roasted scallops top a delicate risotto.
➕ E12 ✉ 1083 côte du Beaver Hall ☎ 514/861-2634 ⏰ Mon–Tue lunch, Wed–Fri lunch and dinner, Sat dinner (call for extended evening opening) 🚇 Square-Victoria

ARIEL ($$$)

www.arielrestaurant.com
The atrium garden of this prettily decorated, three-room restaurant is the perfect place for truffle-scented warm quail and spinach salad.
➕ D12 ✉ 2072 rue Drummond ☎ 514/282-9790 ⏰ Mon, Sat dinner, Tue–Fri lunch and dinner 🚇 Peel
🅿 Reservations

AU BISTRO GOURMET ($$)

www.aubistrogourmet.com
Classic bistro food: duck breast with citrus sauce, mussels in pullet sauce.
➕ C13 ✉ 2100 rue Saint-Mathieu ☎ 514/846-1553 ⏰ Mon–Fri lunch and dinner, Sat–Sun dinner 🚇 Guy-Concordia

BEAVER CLUB ($$$)

www.beaverclub.ca
The Beaver Club is a local institution—it's been here a long time and has a reputation for superior service and stunning presentations. Begin with a trio of foie gras or lobster Charlotte and finish with hot lime soufflé.
➕ E12 ✉ 900 boulevard Rene-Levesque Ouest ☎ 514/861-3511 ext 2448 ⏰ Thu–Sat dinner 🚇 Bonaventure

BEAVER HALL ($$–$$$)

www.beaverhall.ca
Within days of opening, this restaurant became

a firm favorite with the business crowd for its terrific atmosphere and great food, ranging from a succulent burger to artistically presented foie de veau, cuisse de canard or tartare de boeuf.
➕ E12 ✉ 1073 côte du Beaverhall ☎ 514/866-1331 ⏰ Mon–Fri lunch, Sat dinner 🚇 Square-Victoria

BRUTOPIA ($–$$)

www.brutopia.net
This is a great brewpub, with three bars on three floors and terraces outside each. As well as the eight house beers, there's a satisfying menu of international treats, including spicy pan fried dumplings, chorizo nachos, bruschetta, quesadillas and gourmet sandwiches.
➕ D13 ✉ 1219 rue Crescent ☎ 514/393-9277 ⏰ Sat–Thu 3pm–3am, Fri noon–3am 🚇 Lucien L'Allier

CAFE BISTRO ($$)

www.mccord-museum.qc.ca
This is a chic spot in the McCord Museum where local ladies lunch and business deals are sealed. Seafood salad in an avocado is excellent; try maple-nut pie for dessert.
➕ D11 ✉ McCord Museum of Canadian History, 690 rue Sherbrooke Ouest ☎ 514/398-7100 ext 306 ⏰ Tue–Sun 11–4 🚇 McGill

CODE AMBIANCE ($)

www.restaurantambiance.ca
This quirky spot on Antique Row serves

salads, sandwiches and imaginatively sauced pastas. Busy at lunch.
➕ E14 ✉ 1874 rue Notre-Dame Ouest ☎ 514/939-2609 🕐 Mon lunch, Tue–Fri lunch, dinner, Sat dinner 🚇 Lucien-l'Allier

L'ENTRECÔTE SAINT-JEAN ($)
www.lentrecotestjean.com
Bistro decor with a simple and inexpensive menu—walnut salad, sirloin, perfect crunchy fries and chocolate profiteroles.
➕ D12 ✉ 2022 rue Peel ☎ 514/281-6492 🕐 Mon–Fri lunch, dinner, Sat–Sun dinner 🚇 Peel

LA MAISON V.I.P. ($$)
It's far from fancy and it doesn't take reservations, but this Chinatown restaurant serves generous portions of authentic Cantonese dishes to an appreciative crowd of locals who don't mind waiting in line.
➕ F11 ✉ 1077 rue Clark ☎ 514/861-1943 🕐 Daily 11.30am–4am 🚇 Place d'Armes

LE MAS DES OLIVIERS ($$$)
www.lemasdesoliviers.ca
Chef-owner Jacques Muller fills his clients' plates with such deeply satisfying dishes as lamb loin with marrow in port sauce, and tender quail in puff pastry. And the pescadou et sa rouquine, an aromatic fish soup, is superb.

➕ D13 ✉ 1216 rue Bishop ☎ 514/861-6733 🕐 Mon lunch, Tue–Fri lunch, dinner, Sat–Sun dinner 🚇 Guy-Concordia ❓ Reservations

M:BRGR ($$)
www.mbrgr.com
Build your own burger creation, starting with Kobe beef, organic beef, tuna or chicken breast and adding garnishes that range from the prosaic to caramelized onions, cucumber-mango relish or even truffles. The salads are equally good.
➕ D12 ✉ 2025 rue Drummond ☎ 514/906-2747 🕐 Mon–Wed 11.30–10.30, Thu 11.30–11, Fri 11.30am–midnight, Sat noon–midnight, Sun noon–10 🚇 Peel

MR. STEER ($)
www.mistersteer.com
A simple steakhouse with leatherette booths serving great burgers.
➕ D12 ✉ 1198 rue Saint-Catherine Ouest, corner of Drummond ☎ 514/866-3233 🕐 Daily lunch, dinner 🚇 Peel

---

CHEAP EATS

The food courts in the Centre Eaton, Gare Centrale, Complexe Desjardins and Place Ville-Marie are a cut above the usual. Here you'll find stalls selling pastries, Mexican food, grilled sausages and smoked meat, as well as the usual chicken, burgers and fries.

ORCHIDÉE DE CHINE ($$$)
Best of the Tuxedo Chinese restaurants: flash-fried spinach and dumpling with peanut sauce served in an elegantly simple setting.
➕ D12 ✉ 2017 rue Peel ☎ 514/287-1878 🕐 Mon–Fri lunch, dinner, Sat dinner 🚇 Peel

PRESSE CAFÉ ($)
www.pressecafe.com
Good coffee, baked goods, sandwiches and salads, in a bright, cheery setting, with WiFi. Several other outlets around the city.
➕ D12 ✉ 1001 boulevard Maisonneuve Ouest ☎ 514/844-5999 🕐 Daily 6am–7pm 🚇 Peel

RUBY ROUGE ($$)
www.restaurantrubyrouge.com
Very large Chinatown restaurant, popular with Chinese-Canadian and other families, especially at lunch for dim sum. Lotté-Furama is a similar place in the same street at No. 1115 (tel 514/393-3838).
➕ F11 ✉ 1008 rue Clark ☎ 514/390-8828 🕐 Both daily 8am–11pm 🚇 Place d'Armes

LE TAJ ($$)
www.restaurantletaj.com
North Indian specialties, including good tandoori and vegetarian options.
➕ D12 ✉ 2077 rue Stanley, near blvd de Maisonneuve ☎ 514/845-9015 🕐 Mon–Sat lunch, dinner 🚇 Peel

A glorious park protects the heights of Mont-Royal, providing fine walks and sweeping views across the city. Between here and Parc Lafontaine are the Quartier Latin and other lively neighborhoods.

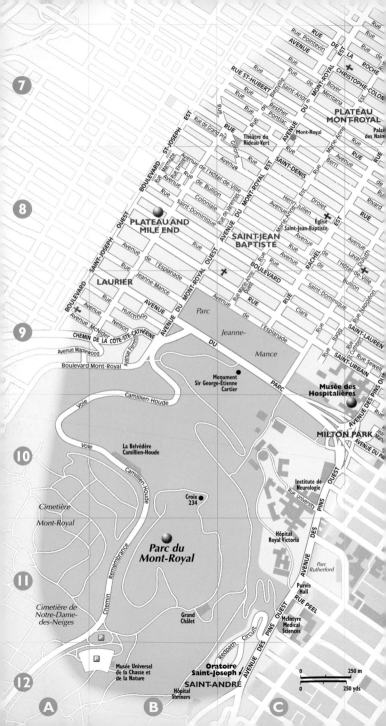

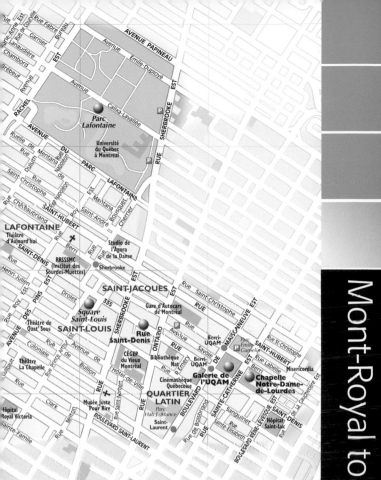

Oratoire Saint-Joseph 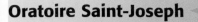 TOP 25

HIGHLIGHTS

● Oratory Museum
● The Primitive Chapel
● Joseph Guardo's eight bas-reliefs
● Gardens of the Way of the Cross

TIPS

● The Oratory Museum is open daily 10–4.30.
● The church has a good caféteria and gift shop.
● You may hear the Petits Chanteurs choir at services on Saturday and Sunday.

The dome of the Oratoire Saint-Joseph, one of the world's largest, is a distinctive landmark, and the church beneath it is the most important Roman Catholic shrine dedicated to Christ's earthly father.

Miracle cures The story begins with Brother André Bessette, a diminutive, barely literate man born in 1837 to a poor rural family. He joined the Congrégation du Saint-Croix and worked as a porter in their college at the foot of Mont-Royal. He built a small shrine to his favorite saint and cared for sick pilgrims, gaining a reputation as a healer. Donations began to pour in from grateful pilgrims to help André fulfill his dream of building a grand monument to Saint Joseph. Construction began in 1924 but Brother André only lived long enough to see the completion of the crypt.

Clockwise from left: Oratoire Saint-Joseph is a striking landmark set against the blue sky; the Primitive Chapel; a sculpture in the Gardens of the Way of the Cross; a statue of the famed healer, Brother André, beneath the dome in the apse

Interior André was beatified in 1982 and buried in the oratory, which also includes part of his original chapel, a small museum, the room in which he died (from a local hospice) and his preserved heart. The 56-bell carillon was originally cast for the Eiffel Tower but was never installed. There are free carillon and organ recitals year-round. Be sure to climb to the observatory for a superb view, and to see the Carrara marble sculptures marking the Stations of the Cross in Mont-Royal.

Development Visitor numbers have increased in the past 20 years from 500,000 to 2 million, and a massive renovation and improvement project is underway. Accessibility is to be improved—already escalators and an elevator have been installed—and further work will restore existing parts, add new buildings and improve landscaping.

THE BASICS

www.saint-joseph.org

✚ Off map at A13

✉ 3800 chemin Queen Mary, near Côte-des-Neiges

☎ 514/733-8211 or 877/672-8647

⊙ Late Jun–Aug daily 6.30am–9.30pm; Sep–late-Jun daily 7am–9pm

🍽 Café

Ⓜ Côte-des-Neiges

🚌 51, 165, 166

♿ Very good

👐 Oratory free. Museum guided tours inexpensive

71

HIGHLIGHTS

- Montréal Cross
- Le Chalet viewpoint
- Beaver Lake
- Smith House
- Mont-Royal Cemetery

TIP

- Energetic visitors can rent bicycles, skates, snowshoes, Nordic skis and kick-sleds, inner tubes (a bouncy alternative to toboggans) and pedal boats.

Mont-Royal is only 233m (764ft) above sea level but Montréalers call it, without irony, "the Mountain," an appropriately grand appellation given the hold this steep, green oasis has on their affection.

Park on the hill Mont-Royal is one of seven such peaks on the Saint Lawrence plain, all composed of intrusive rock hard enough to have survived the glacial erosion of the last Ice Age. Explorer Jacques Cartier named the hill—probably in honor of his royal patron, François I of France— on his first voyage up the Saint Lawrence in 1535. The area became a park in 1876, amid fears that the forested slopes were being denuded for firewood. The land was bought for $1 million, and landscaped by Frederick Law Olmsted, also responsible for New York's Central Park.

Clockwise from left: Beaver Lake, created in the 1930s; there are spectacular views of Montréal from Le Chalet, during the day or when the city lights come on; jogging along the shore of Beaver Lake

So much to do The park is too large to see in a day, so pick a corner to explore. Most people on foot enter at the Monument Sir George-Étienne Cartier, a popular summer venue for street musicians, vendors and people-watchers. Olmsted Road leads to the Montréal Cross (1924) on the summit. Beaver Lake, created in the 1930s, is another focal point, as is Le Chalet, which has fantastic views from its Belvédère Kondiaronk. The Smith House, dating from 1858, is the park's Welcome Centre, with an exhibition about the park's history and ecology, an information point, gift shop and café. There are two cemeteries on the northern edge that offer surprisingly pleasant strolls (look for the grave of Ann Leonowens, immortalized in *The King and I*, in the Mont-Royal Cemetery). In winter, rent skis, skates, snowshoes and kick-sleds at the park.

THE BASICS

www.lemontroyal.qc.ca

🞢 B11

✉ Entrances off avenue du Parc, avenue des Pins and elsewhere

☎ 514/843-8240

🕐 Park daily 6am–midnight; Smith House Mon–Fri 9–6, Sat–Sun 10–6 (winter hours vary)

🍽 The Chalet, Café Smith

Ⓜ Mont-Royal, then bus to top

🚌 11, 80, 129, 165, 535

♿ Some steep paths

▮ Free

73

Plateau and Mile End

TOP 25

Bernard Street in the Mile End district (left); bagels on sale (right)

THE BASICS

🔲 D7/B8
🔲 Mont-Royal, Laurier

HIGHLIGHTS

- Vernacular architecture
- St-Viateur Bagel bakery
- Avenue Mont-Royal
- Avenue Laurier

Home to young professionals and creative types, these neighborhoods are packed with individual boutiques and vibrant bars, restaurants and live music venues. On summer evenings the residential streets have a great buzz, with everyone socializing on their balconies.

Blue-collar origins Dating from the Industrial Revolution and originally built for working-class families, the two- or three-floor row-houses that line the streets contain separate apartments on each floor. Their outdoor staircases and balconies serve a dual purpose, giving each apartment a private external door and, with no need for internal staircases, providing more living space inside.

Plateau The Plateau lies north of rue Sherbrooke to the east of Parc du Mont-Royal. Its main commercial thoroughfares are avenue du Mont-Royal and rue Saint-Denis, both lined by individual boutiques and specialty stores, restaurants and cafés. Place Gérald-Godin and rue Prince-Arthur (pedestrian-only in summer) are lively spots, with street entertainers in summer.

Mile End Strictly part of the borough of Plateau-Mont-Royal, Mile End is quite distinct, more multicultural and less prettified. It has attracted not only artists and musicians but also stars of the computer graphics generation and is a place for the in-crowd to hang out. The most chic shopping is around avenue Laurier and boulevard Saint-Laurent, again packed with one-of-a-kind stores.

CHAPELLE NOTRE-DAME-DE-LOURDES

www.cndlm.org

The Quartier Latin's Our Lady of Lourdes Chapel faces the old church of Saint-Jacques, hidden behind a bland exterior. But its sumptuously decorated interior, a mixture of Romanesque and Byzantine styles that dates from 1876, has vivid murals—the work of artist Napoléon Bourassa.

✚ F9 ⊠ 430 rue Sainte-Catherine Est ☎ 514/842-4704 ⏰ Mon–Fri 11–6, Sat 10.30–6.30, Sun 9–6.30 Ⓜ Berri-UQAM

GALERIE DE L'UQAM

www.galerie.uqam.ca

The strength of this modern gallery resulted in it being chosen to represent Canada at the 2007 Venice Biennale. The gallery was established as part of the Université du Québec à Montréal (UQAM) in 1975 with the collection from the former school of fine arts. It has expanded considerably, but the real emphasis here is on engaging both students and visitors with a thought-provoking schedule of temporary exhibitions. The gallery's emphasis is on contemporary art.

✚ F9 ⊠ Université du Québec à Montréal, 1400 rue Berri ☎ 514/987-8421 ⏰ Tue–Sat 12–6 Ⓜ Berri-UQAM Ⓦ Free

MUSÉE DES HOSPITALIÈRES

www.museedeshospitalieres.qc.ca

The museum tells the story of the Hôtel-Dieu, Montréal's first hospital, and the Hospitalières de Saint-Joseph, recruited in France in 1659 by Montréal's co-founder, Jeanne Mance. The displays also deal with the working lives of the medical staff, their training and the treatments they administered, their religious inspiration and the history of medicine. There are also regular temporary exhibitions, drawing on aspects of the collection of 20,000 artifacts and documents held here.

✚ D10 ⊠ 201 avenue des Pins Ouest ☎ 514/849-2919 ⏰ Mid-Jun to mid-Oct Tue–Fri 10–5, Sat–Sun 1–5; mid-Oct to mid-Jun Wed–Sun 1–5 Ⓜ Sherbrooke 🚌 144 ♿ Fair Ⓦ Moderate

Chapelle Notre-Dame-de-Lourdes

PARC LAFONTAINE

This beautiful park is a large expanse of green within the Plateau neighborhood, and residents and visitors alike make full use of it. Its summer appeal is obvious, with its two linked ponds, lawns to lounge on, the cycle path and playing fields; in winter there's skating and hockey. Lafontaine divides into an English-style landscape in the west and a French-style garden in the east, with tennis courts, outdoor swimming pools and summer concerts.

🔁 E7 ☒ Avenue du Parc Lafontaine, between Sherbrooke Est and Rachel 🕐 Daily 9am–10pm 🍴 Snack bar 🚇 Sherbrooke 🚌 14, 24, 29 ♿ Good 🎫 Free

RUE SAINT-DENIS

Rue Saint-Denis bisects Montréal's Latin Quarter and is a colorful and picturesque mix of interesting architecture and chic boutiques, some looking as if they occupy the front parlor of someone's house. Up outside staircases or dipping down into the basement of an old stone building there's an appealing mix of haute-couture boutiques, designer homewares, individualistic music stores, antiques shops, arts, crafts and gifts. There are plenty of cafés, bistros and restaurants for weary shoppers too. The nightlife is good here, too, with lots of bars and pubs, and there's the Théâtre d'Aujourd'hui, which showcases cutting-edge works by Québec playwrights.

🔁 E9 🚇 Berri-UQAM, Sherbrooke

SQUARE SAINT-LOUIS

This leafy square was laid out in 1879 and is considered one of the city's finest. Its beautiful houses—very French-looking—are now home to poets, artists and writers attracted by the bohemian atmosphere of the surrounding Latin Quarter. It's some of the most expensive real estate in the city. The square's centerpiece is a fine Victorian fountain. At its southern end, rue Prince-Arthur Est is full of street entertainers in summer, when it is closed to motor vehicles.

🔁 E9 🚇 Sherbrooke

Parc Lafontaine has two linked ponds

Parks and Views

A walk that offers a taste of Montréal's loveliest park and provides a majestic overview of the city from its various panoramic lookouts.

DISTANCE: 5–7km (3–4 miles)   **ALLOW:** 2–3 hours

START

MONUMENT SIR GEORGE ÉTIENNE CARTIER ⊞ C9 🚇 Mont-Royal

1 Take a cab to the Monument Sir George-Étienne Cartier, a popular spot and the main northern entrance to Parc du Mont-Royal (▷ 72).

2 Follow the looping chemin Olmsted up through the park, a 4.8km (3-mile) gravel path created by the park's designer to accommodate horse-drawn carriages.

3 At several points in the park you can see the Montréal Cross (Croix sur la Montagne; ▷ 73), a landmark erected in 1924 and visible across the city.

4 About midway up the chemin Olmsted, 200 steps provide a short-cut to Le Chalet du Mont-Royal. Take this if you are fit, but otherwise continue on the chemin Olmsted.

END

RUE DES PINS OUEST ⊞ C11 🚇 Peel

8 From here you can walk to sights such as the Musée McCord d'Histoire Canadienne (▷ 55), McGill University (▷ 52–53) or the Musée des Beaux-Arts (▷ 54).

7 At the end of the chemin Olmsted, the rustic Chalet offers another café and superb views over the city. Retrace your steps, or take the steps, and follow Redpath Crescent to rue des Pins Ouest.

6 Above the lake, walk through the sculpture garden to the Maison Smith, which has a visitor center and café.

5 The path curves round to a grassy area around Lac-des-Castors (Beaver Lake), a popular place for summer and winter activities.

Shopping

AIME COM MOI

www.aimecommoi.com
A great boutique for the latest in exclusive high-quality fashions for women, mostly from Montréal and Québec-based designers.
🚩 C8 ✉ 150 avenue du Mont-Royal Est ☎ 514/982-0088 🕐 Mon–Wed 11–7, Thu, Fri 11–7, Sat 11–5, Sun 12–5 🚇 Mont-Royal

ARCHAMBAULT

www.archambault.ca
Montréal's own music shop is excellent for current releases, classical music and Québec pop. It also has an extensive selection of song books and sheet music.
🚩 E10 ✉ 175 rue Sainte-Catherine Est ☎ 514/849-8589 🕐 Mon–Fri 9.30–9, Sat 9–5, Sun 10–5 🚇 Berri-UQAM

BELLA PELLA

www.bellapella.com
Bella Pella is Italian for "Beautiful Skin," and this scented shop sells lotions, potions, soaps, shampoos and other body-care products, most of them made with organic products by small, local producers.
🚩 C7 ✉ 1201A avenue du Mont-Royal Est ☎ 514/904-1074 🕐 Mon–Wed 11–6, Thu, Fri 11–9, Sat 11–5, Sun 12–5 🚇 Mont-Royal

CHAPOFOLIE

Both men and women can complete their fashion purchases here, at the largest hat store in the city.
🚩 D9 ✉ 3944 rue Saint-Denis C514/982-0036 🕐 Mon–Thu 11–6, Fri 11–9, Sat 11–5, Sun 1–5 🚇 Sherbrooke

LES COURS MONT-ROYAL

www.lcmr.ca
This elegant shopping center is in the old Mount Royal Hotel, a jazz-age palace that was the largest hotel in the British Empire when it opened in 1922. When developers gutted the place in 1987, they left the exterior intact and saved part of the old lobby, complete with a crystal chandelier that used to illuminate the Monte Carlo Casino. The inner court rises 10 floors to the roof, and is surrounded by balconies and fashionable shops.
🚩 D12 ✉ 1550 rue Metcalfe ☎ 514/842-7777 🚇 Peel

FURS

Montréal owes its early commercial success to the fur trades. Despite trends away from the wearing of furs, the city still boasts some of Canada's best furriers. Grosvenor-McComber (✉ 9250 avenue du Parc ☎ 514/288-1255) has been in business since 1895. Birger Christensen at Holt Renfrew (✉ 1300 rue Sherbrooke Ouest ☎ 514/842-5111) is a favorite among the city elite.

DÉPART EN MER

www.departenmer.com
Everything nautical, including exquisite ship models, fine antiques, art, brasses and yacht wear.
🚩 D9 ✉ 4306 rue Saint-Denis ☎ 514/288-6273 🕐 Mon–Wed 11–6, Thu, Fri 11–7, Sat 11–5, Sun 12–5 🚇 Sherbrooke

DUBUC MODE DE VIE

www.dubucstyle.com
Philippe Dubuc is one of Canada's premier designers of men's and women's clothes. This stylish boutique is his headquarters and displays both collections.
🚩 D9 ✉ 4451 rue Saint-Denis ☎ 514/282-1465 🕐 Mon–Wed 10.30–6 Thu, Fri 10.30–9, Sat 10.30–5, Sun 1–5 🚇 Mont-Royal

FAIRMOUNT BAGEL BAKERY

www.fairmountbagel.com
Montréal is famous for its bagels and this is one of the two most famous producers. This one is the oldest, established in 1919, and it makes more than 20 varieties, all hand-rolled and cooked in a wood-fired oven.
🚩 A8 ✉ 74 rue Fairmount Ouest ☎ 514/272-0667 🕐 Daily 24 hours 🚇 Laurier

GENERAL 54 AND LOCAL 23

http://general54.blogspot.com
Funky accessories and jewelry are on offer at these twin stores. The work of more than 30

designers and artists is showcased, including the clothing line of co-owner Jen Glasgow.

➕ A7 ✉ 54 rue Saint-Viateur Ouest ☎ 514/271-2129 🕐 General 54: Sat–Wed 12–6, Thu, Fri 12–7. Local 23: Tue, Wed 12–6, Thu, Fri 12–7, Sat, Sun 12–6 🚇 Laurier

KALIYANA

http://kaliyana.com

Stylish and interesting, easy to wear yet innovative, the women's clothing comes in a realistic range of sizes (6 to 24). They have some very unconventional footwear, too.

➕ D8 ✉ 4107 rue Saint-Denis ☎ 514/844-0633 🕐 Mon–Wed 10.30–6, Thu, Fri 10.30–8, Sat 10–5, Sun 11–5 🚇 Mont Royal, Sherbrooke

KANUK

www.kanuk.com

Here you can uncover everything you need for when the temperature drops. The coats, sleeping bags and items are widely available, but you'll find the keenest prices here at the factory store, where there is a big sale in November.

➕ D8 ✉ 485 rue Rachel Est ☎ 514/284-4494 or 877/284-4494 🕐 Mon–Wed 9–6, Thu, Fri 9–9, Sat 10–5, Sun 12–5 🚇 Mont-Royal 🚌 30

POTERIE MANU REVA

www.poteriemanureva.com

This Mile End gem stocks the work of 27 local potters and includes a wide range of decorative as well as usable items.

➕ B8 ✉ 5141 boulevard Saint-Laurent ☎ 514/948-1717 🕐 Tue–Fri 12–6, Sat 10–5 🚇 Laurier

ST-VIATEUR BAGEL

www.stviateurbagel.com

Established in 1957, this is Montréal's other landmark bagel bakery. Shunning innovation, they have only ever made two varieties—sesame and poppy seed—and drop the hand-rolled dough into hot water before baking in the wood oven. Other branches, with cafés, are located at 1127 avenue du Mont-Royal Est and 5629 avenue Monkland.

➕ A8 ✉ 263 avenue Saint-Viateur Ouest ☎ 514/276-8044 or 866/662-2435 🕐 Daily 24 hours 🚇 Laurier

---

WHERE TO LOOK

Antiques hunters with thick wallets search for treasures in the lavish shops along rue Sherbrooke Ouest and in exclusive Westmount. The more modest crowd look on trendy Antique Alley on rue Notre-Dame Ouest. Real hunters haunt the shops on rue Amherst, where they can buy wooden toys in Antiquités Curiosités at No. 1769, or scavenge chrome fittings from the 1950s in Cité Déco at No. 1761.

TONY PAPPAS

www.tonypappas.ca

Established in 1900, this shoe shop is a refreshing change from the chains downtown. It stocks international quality footwear from the likes of Clarks and Hush Puppies, and also Québec-made styles. It also has a first-class traditional repair shop.

➕ D6 ✉ 1822 avenue Mont-Royal Est ☎ 514/521-0820 🕐 Mon–Wed 8.30–6, Thu–Fri 8.30–9, Sat 8.30–5, Sun 12–5 🚇 Mont-Royal

VALET D'COEUR

www.levalet.com

This is a shop for children and adults of all ages, and sells an excellent range of board games, comics, posters and toys. Its range of chess sets and boards is second to none.

➕ C8 ✉ 4408 rue Saint-Denis ☎ 514/499-9970 🕐 Mon–Wed 10–6, Thu–Fri 10–9, Sat 10–5, Sun 12–5 🚇 Mont-Royal

WAXMAN

www.waxman.ca

Long-established purveyor of formal menswear in a very elegant showroom. You can get made-to-measure or off-the-peg tuxedos, vests and accessories, or rent something if you arrived in town unprepared.

➕ B9 ✉ 4605 avenue du Parc ☎ 514/845-8826 🕐 Mon–Wed 9–6, Thu–Fri 9–9, Sat 9–5 🚇 Mont-Royal

Entertainment and Nightlife

APARTMENT 200
Loft-style space with a bar, DJs and dancing.
✚ D9 ✉ 3643 boulevard Saint-Laurent ☎ 514/282-7665 🕐 Thu–Sat 10.30pm–3am 🚇 Saint-Laurent

LE BALATTOU
www.balattou.com
A welcoming (if hot and crowded) dance club with an African and tropical motif.
✚ C8 ✉ 4372 boulevard Saint-Laurent ☎ 514/845-5447 🕐 Tue–Sun 9pm–3am 🚌 29, 55

BELMONT ON THE BOULEVARD
www.lebelmont.com
Quiet bar with plenty of room to sit and talk. A disco is to the rear. Lines on weekends.
✚ C8 ✉ 4483 boulevard Saint-Laurent ☎ 514/845-8443 🕐 Thu–Sat 9pm–3am 💰 Cover charge on weekends 🚇 Saint-Laurent, Mont-Royal 🚌 29, 55

BILY KUN
www.bilykun.com
This is a cool Plateau hang-out. Come early evening for jazz (Tue–Fri) or classical music (Sun), or after 10pm any night for DJ music.
✚ C8 ✉ 354 avenue du Mont-Royal Est ☎ 514/845-5392 🕐 Daily 3pm–3am 🚇 Mont-Royal

BISTRO A JOJO
www.bistroajojo.com
A relaxed and intimate blues club that's been in business since 1975. Come early to be sure of one of the simple wooden chairs at the close-packed tables. Great people-watching on the sidewalk terrace.
✚ E9 ✉ 1627 rue Saint-Denis ☎ 514/843-5015 🕐 Shows Wed–Sun from 10pm 🚇 Berri-UQAM

LE CHEVAL BLANC
wordp.lechevalblanc.ca
Unchanged for 25 years, music combines with the buzz of arty and political talk. Communal tables; beer brewed on-site.
✚ E9 ✉ 809 rue Ontario Est ☎ 514/522-0211 🕐 Daily 3pm–3am 🚇 Berri-UQAM

LE CLUB SODA
www.clubsoda.ca
This is an excellent venue where you can be sure to find good live music (including big international names) and other shows, such as comedy.

WHERE TO GO?
Clubs and discos are notorious for fading in and out of fashion, or for closing down altogether, so for the latest on clubs check the free magazines to be found at tourist offices, record shops and cafés. *The Mirror, the Hour* and the French *Voir* (all free) contain extensive listings of clubs and live music venues, as does *The Montréal Gazette*, the city's main English-language newspaper.

✚ E10 ✉ 1225 boulevard Saint-Laurent ☎ 514/286-1010 🕐 Daily 8pm–2am 🚇 Saint-Laurent

DIESE ONZE JAZZ CLUB
www.dieseonze.com
Nightly live jazz, and often also an opener for the after-work crowd in this intimate basement. Tapas and light main plates are served, too, at reasonable prices.
✚ D8 ✉ 4115 rue Saint-Denis ☎ 514/223-3543 🕐 Daily from 5pm 🚇 Sherbrooke

MME LEE
A sleek contemporary lounge-club with numerous cocktails and tapas-style snacks on offer.
✚ E9 ✉ 151 rue Ontario Est ☎ 514/285-2621 🕐 Tue–Fri 5pm–3am, Sat 9pm–3am 🚇 Saint-Laurent

LE PASSEPORT
www.barpasseport.com
A long-running club with good music.
✚ D8 ✉ 2037 rue Saint-Denis ☎ 514/286-6166 🕐 Wed, Fri, Sat 10pm–3am 🚇 Sherbrooke, Mont-Royal

QUAI DES BRUMES
www.quaidesbrumes.ca
This intimate neighborhood jazz club has been in business for over 25 years. Performances are lively and creative.
✚ C8 ✉ 4481 rue Saint-Denis ☎ 514/499-0467 🕐 Daily 2pm–3am 🚇 Mont-Royal

PRICES

Prices are approximate, based on a 3-course meal for one person.

$$$	over $40
$$	$20–$40
$	under $20

À LA DÉCOUVERTE ($$)

Classic French cuisine on a quiet street. Reserve two weeks in advance for weekends. Reservations essential. BYOB.

🚆 C7 ✉ 4350 rue de la Roche ☎ 514/529-8377 ⏰ Thu–Sat dinner 🚇 Mont-Royal 1

AU PIED DE COCHON ($$)

www.restaurantaupiedde cochon.ca

The Pig's Foot offers robust dishes guaranteed to warm on a cold day, with fish and lighter dishes in summer.

🚆 D8 ✉ 536 avenue Duluth ☎ 514/281-1114 ⏰ Dinner daily 🚇 Sherbrooke, Mont-Royal

BISTROT LA FABRIQUE ($$$)

www.bistrolafabrique.com

Reserve a middle table to watch one of the city's rising stars prepare your dinner, and feast on Jean-Baptiste Marchand's potato gnocchi with snails, seared foie gras with preserved duck and mushroom duxelle, or beef and wild mushroom tart with aged cheddar.

Don't miss his signature French toast for dessert.

🚆 C8 ✉ 3609 rue Saint-Denis ☎ 514/544-5038 ⏰ Dinner daily (opens 10.30am Sun) 🚇 Sherbrooke

BON BLÉ RIZ ($$)

Lamb in a peppery anise-flavored sauce and spicy shrimp are among the flamboyant dishes at this unpretentious Chinese restaurant.

🚆 E10 ✉ 1437 boulevard Saint-Laurent ☎ 514/844-1447 ⏰ Mon–Fri lunch, dinner, Sat dinner 🚇 Saint-Laurent

LA BRIOCHE LYONNAISE ($)

www.labriochelyonnaise.com

A classic pâtisserie in a city known for its cakes and confectioners. The chocolates are fabulous.

🚆 E9 ✉ 1593 rue Saint-Denis, between boulevard de Maisonneuve and rue Emery ☎ 514/842-7017 ⏰ Daily breakfast, lunch, dinner 🚇 Berri-UQAM

CAFÉ FERREIRA ($$$)

www.ferreiracafe.com

Haute cuisine Portuguese style. Nibble on salted cod and olives while you consider the grilled octopus or the sausages marinated in red wine.

🚆 D12 ✉ 1446 rue Peel ☎ 514/848-0988 ⏰ Mon–Fri lunch, dinner, Sat dinner 🚇 Peel ❓ Reserve ahead

CAFÉ SANTROPOL ($)

www.santropol.com

A charming student café with mainly vegetarian food, and more than 60 herbal teas. Many ice creams, malts and sodas, and plenty of fruit juices, salads and quiches.

🚆 C9 ✉ 3990 rue Saint-Urbain ☎ 514/842-3110 ⏰ Daily 11.30–10.30 🚇 Sherbrooke

DANS LA BOUCHE ($–$$)

www.danslabouche.ca

Brunch place with a good atmosphere and wonderful eggs Benedict and other breakfast specialties; also good tapas. There are two other Montréal outlets.

🚆 D6 ✉ 2000 avenue du Mont-Royal Est ☎ 514/526-1401 ⏰ Daily 6am–11pm 🚇 Mont-Royal

L'EXPRESS ($$)

www.restaurantlexpress.ca

Parisian-style bistro with a zinc bar, elbow-to-elbow tables, cheerfully frantic service, perfect food and interesting wines.

🚆 D8 ✉ 3927 rue Saint-Denis at rue Duluth ☎ 514/845-5333 ⏰ Mon–Fri 8am–2am, Sat 10am–2am, Sun 10am–1am 🚇 Sherbrooke ❓ Reservations essential

LE JARDIN DE PANOS ($$)

www.lejardindepanos.com

Greek restaurant with popular dishes such as moussaka.

🚆 D8 ✉ 521 rue Duluth Est ☎ 514/521-4206 ⏰ Daily lunch, dinner 🚇 Sherbrooke, Mont-Royal

LALOUX ($$)

www.laloux.com
Classic French food with a modern edge in a discreet, elegant setting.
🔳 D9 ✉ 250 avenue des Pins Est ☎ 514/287-9127
🕔 Mon–Fri lunch, dinner, Sat, Sun dinner 🚇 Sherbrooke
🅿 Reservations

MAIKO SUSHI ($$)

www.maiko-sushi.com
Artistic sushi, prepared before your eyes at the sushi bar, is served in chic surroundings. There's a good choice of teriyaki, seafood and dishes such as grilled rack of lamb and *filet mignon*. Or you can order from a selection of complete meals.
🔳 Off map A8 ✉ 387 rue Bernard Ouest ☎ 514/490-1225 🕔 Mon–Fri lunch, dinner, Sat–Sun dinner
🚇 Outremont

MOISHE'S ($)

www.moishes.ca
Eat marbled steak aged the same way since 1938. A premier steak house, run by the same family since it opened. Crowded and noisy.
🔳 C9 ✉ 3961 boulevard Saint-Laurent at rue Duluth ☎ 514/845-3509 🕔 Daily dinner 🚇 Saint-Laurent, then bus 55 north

OMNIVORE ($$$)

www.omnigrill.com
An informal counter-service restaurant with a Mediterranean and Middle Eastern flavor that offers excellent grilled and other meats (all organic), as well as snacks, sandwiches, specials up on the blackboard and a good choice for vegetarians and vegans (hence the name).
🔳 C9 ✉ 4351 boulevard Saint-Laurent at rue Marie-Anne ☎ 514/303-5757
🕔 Mon–Sat 11–10 🚇 Mont-Royal

PHAYA THAI ($)

www.phayathailaurier.com
This Thai restaurant is typical of the ever-increasing range of ethnic cuisines available in Montréal.
🔳 B8 ✉ 107 avenue Laurier Ouest ☎ 514/272-3456
🕔 Mon–Fri 11–2.30, Sun–Wed 5pm–10pm 🚇 Laurier

PSAROTAVERNA DU SYMPOSIUM ($$)

Enjoy grilled fresh fish, shrimp and octopus.
🔳 D8 ✉ 3829 rue Saint-Denis ☎ 514/842-0867

BRING YOUR OWN BOTTLE

If you're watching your budget, consider dining at a restaurant that allows you to bring your own wine. Entries are designated as "BYOB"—bring your own bottle (*Apporter son vin*). BYOB restaurants are common in Montréal, thanks to a quirk in Québec's provincial liquor laws. The food quality in these places ranges from pedestrian to excellent, but is usually inexpensive.

🕔 Mon–Fri lunch, dinner, Sat dinner 🚇 Sherbrooke

SCHWARTZ'S ($)

The best thing on the menu is smoked meat but the steaks are pretty good too. Famous and packed, expect brusque service and lines.
🔳 D9 ✉ 3895 boulevard Saint-Laurent at rue Napoléon ☎ 514/842-4813 🕔 Daily lunch, dinner 🚇 Mont-Royal

SU SHIAN YUANG ($)

A charming and under-stated place offering inexpensive and perfectly cooked Chinese food (eat off the menu, not the set meals), with many vegetarian and gluten-free options. Menus vary, but the soups are generally good, and if it is available, try the *pai gu* (vegetarian spare ribs made from crispy wheat and taro).
🔳 D8 ✉ 420 rue Rachel-East at rue Saint-Denis ☎ 514/380 2829 🕔 Mon–Fri lunch, dinner, Sat dinner 🚇 Mont-Royal

UNIBURGER ($)

Uniburger replaced the much-loved La Paryse, a touchstone for gourmet burgers in the city for years. But the newcomer's food has also won plaudits, with fresh ingredients, a casual setting and a simple menu. Popular with students at the nearby junior college.
🔳 E9 ✉ 302 rue Ontario Est ☎ 514/419-6555 🕔 Mon–Sat 11–9 🚇 Berri-UQAM

The striking stadium and buildings created for the 1976 Olympic Games, along with the Jardin Botanique, one of the world's largest botanical gardens, provide a fine counterpart to Montréal's other attractions.

Maisonneuve and Le Village

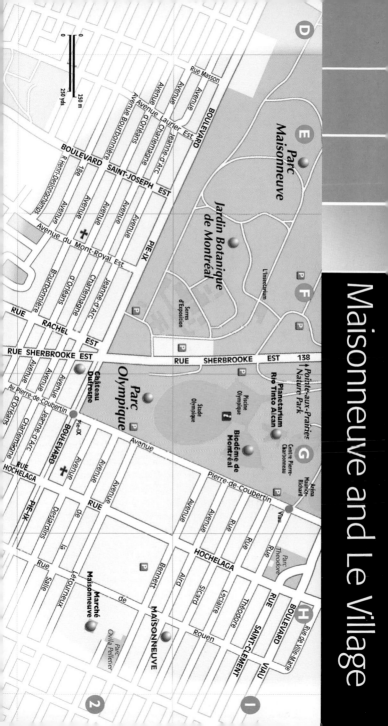

Maisonneuve and Le Village

Biodôme de Montréal

TOP 25

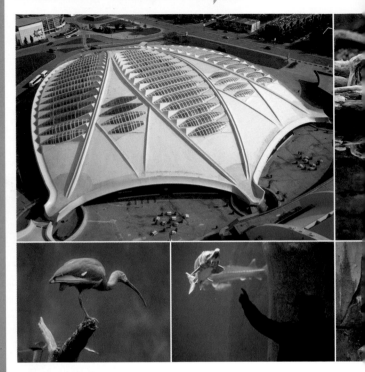

HIGHLIGHTS

● The sloths in the rainforest
● The beaver dam and lodge in the Saint Lawrence habitat
● Puffins and penguins in the Arctic and Antarctic areas

TIPS

● Use the free shuttle bus to travel between the Biodôme, Parc Olympique, Viau Métro, Insectarium and Jardin Botanique (mid-May to late October).
● Rent binoculars at the Biodôme for close-up views.

The Biodôme has been a success ever since it opened in 1992 in what used to be the Olympic velodrome. This living museum integrates birds, animals and plants into superb re-creations of their natural habitats.

Habitats Montréal's Biodôme, the only one of its kind in the world, replicates four of the most beautiful habitats in North, Central and South America—tropical forest, the Saint Lawrence marine ecosystem, Laurentian forest, and the Arctic and Antarctic—with their plants, birds, marine creatures and other animals. You watch otters frolicking in waterfalls, observe marine creatures through glass and peek at animals and preening birds through the foliage of living forest. But this is more than an indoor zoo. It is actively involved in

Clockwise from left: Montréal's Biodôme contains four ecosystems; a visitor watches the fish; the huge globe provides a central point to touch base; a tamarin in the tropical forest; a penguin looks around; watching a fish in the Saint Lawrence marine ecosystem; a brightly colored resident of the tropical forest

breeding endangered species in captivity with the hope of releasing the offspring into the wild.

Animals As you walk into the first habitat, the Amazonian rainforest, heat, humidity and animal smells hit you like a wall. Exotic birds chirp overhead, while the leafy undergrowth is alive with crocodiles, capybaras and golden lion tamarins (orange-furred monkeys that are increasingly scarce in their native Brazil). You'll also see darting parrots, a cave full of bats (behind glass) and other mammals, amphibians, reptiles and fish. In the Laurentian forest you can watch lynx, otter, beaver and porcupine. A tank in the Saint Lawrence marine ecosystem re-creates a sea, complete with nesting gannets and a tidal pool filled with sea urchins and anemones. There are popular puffins and penguins in the Arctic and Antarctic areas.

THE BASICS

espacepourlavie.ca
✚ G1
✉ 4777 avenue Pierre-de-Coubertin
☎ 514/868-3000
🕐 Late Jun–early Sep daily 9–6. Early Sep–late Jun Tue–Sun 9–5
🍴 Café
🚇 Viau
♿ Very good
✋ Expensive. Combined tickets available with Jardin Botanique
❓ Gift shop

Jardin Botanique de Montréal

HIGHLIGHTS

- Summer butterflies
- Tropical greenhouse gardens (open year-round)
- Orchids and begonias
- First Nations garden
- The Rose Garden
- The Chinese Garden

TIPS

- Check ahead for times of the tea ceremonies in the Japanese Garden Pavilion and the *Croque Insectes*.
- Leave enough time for the Arboretum, it covers a big area.

Montréal has the world's second-largest botanical gardens—no small feat given the cruel climate. The preserve is a blend of exotic horticulture with the beauty and tranquility of a formal garden.

Gardens Opened in 1931, Montréal's lovely botanical gardens comprise some 30 different outdoor gardens and 10 vast exhibition greenhouses. Each garden and glasshouse represents a different climate, country or style, ranging from a collection of poisonous plants to gardens devoted to orchids or medicinal herbs. Nearby lies the Insectarium, in a bug-shape building. Its galleries are filled with displays of countless insects living and dead (and exotic butterflies in summer). Don't miss the gargantuan South American cockroaches. In February visitors can try

Clockwise from left: bonsai trees in the Japanese Garden; a wider view of the Japanese Garden; a pavilion in the Montréal-Shanghai Dream Lake Garden; sun shining through the trees in the arboretum; maple leaves, a symbol of Canada

some high-protein morsels as local cooks whip up chocolate-covered ants, honey-dipped bees and the ever-popular bug-centered lollipops.

Shanghai surprise The gardens' highlight is the 2ha (6-acre) Montréal-Shanghai Dream Lake Garden (The Chinese Garden), a perfect replica of one from the Ming dynasty (1368–1644) designed to celebrate the friendship between the two cities. Lakes, rocks and plants strive for a harmonious blend of yin and yang: small and large, soft and hard, light and dark, flowing and immovable. Look for the seven pavilions, central reflecting pool, rockery and collection of miniature trees known as "pen-jings" (displayed in a greenhouse in winter). The Japanese Garden and Pavilion are exquisite, as is the summer collection of bonsai trees.

THE BASICS

espacepourlavie.ca

➕ F1

✉ 4101 rue Sherbrooke Est

☎ 514/ 872-1400

🕐 Late Jun–early Sep daily 9–6; early Sep Oct daily 9–9; Nov–late Jun daily 9–5

🍴 Café

🚇 Viau, Pie-IX

🚌 185

♿ Very good

💲 Expensive (includes Insectarium). Parking fee

❓ Free shuttle bus from Le Biodôme, Parc Olympique and Viau Métro

Parc Olympique

The Montréal Tower (opposite) and a view from the top (right); Olympic Stadium (left)

During the summer 1976 Olympic Games, the perfect performances of Romanian gymnast Nadia Comaneci thrilled the world. But once over, the games left an architectural and financial legacy that still divides the city.

Soaring costs When Mayor Jean Drapeau persuaded Montréalers to host the Olympic Games in 1976 he promised that the event wouldn't cost them a cent. French architect Roger Taillibert set to work, believing money was no object. Both were wrong. The stadium and its tower cost $1.2 (US) billion, but it has never been much of a success as a sports venue, abandoned by the local football team, and the Expos, Montréal's major league baseball team, after the franchise moved. The place makes its money on trade shows and huge concerts. But it's impressively bright and airy, and worth seeing.

Leaning tower It is not so much the stadium that pulls in visitors, it's the park's famous inclined tower (Tour de Montréal), built to support the stadium's retractable roof. Since it opened in 1989, more than 5 million people have ascended to the observation platform. The 175m (575ft) ascent via an external cable car is stomach churning, but you are rewarded with a view that on a clear day stretches for 80km (50 miles). Galleries in the tower's lower levels contain displays about the park's history, and the Tourist Hall at the tower's base has information, tickets and exhibits.

THE BASICS

parcolympique.qc.ca

⊞ G2

✉ 4141 avenue Pierre-de-Coubertin

☎ 514/252-4141 or 877/997-0919

🕐 Mid-Jun to early Sep daily 9–7; early Sep to mid-Jun Tue–Sun 9–6, Mon 1–5. Closed early Jan to mid-Feb

🍴 Café (summer only)

🚇 Viau or Pie-IX (free shuttle from Viau mid-May to late Oct 11–5)

🚌 185

♿ Very good

💲 Tower: expensive. Tours: moderate

❓ Souvenir shop

TIPS

● Use the sports center, with various fitness classes and open sessions in the swimming pool and badminton courts.

● Regular 30-minute guided tours ($8 adult, $6.25 child) leave from the base of the Tour de Montréal from 10am May–Aug and 11am Sep–Apr.

More to See

CHÂTEAU DUFRESNE

www.chateaudufresne.qc.ca

Little in the symmetrical Beaux-Arts facade of this building suggests that it is two buildings, built between 1915 and 1918 for brothers Marius and Oscar Dufresne. Marius, the architect, lived in the west wing and his brother in the east wing. When the Dufresne families moved on, the house became a boys' school in the 1950s under the guardianship of priests, who covered many of the racier friezes and murals. Many have been rediscovered, along with much of the original interiors, offering a vivid insight into the lives of Montréal's Francophone elite at the beginning of the 20th century. An exhibition places the house in context, but it is the sumptuous interiors that prove most compelling, with marble staircases, gold-damask hangings, mahogany-covered walls, stained-glass windows and beautiful coffered ceilings.

➕ F2 ✉ 2929 avenue Jeanne-d'Arc ☎ 514/259-9201 🕐 Wed–Sun 10–5 🚇 Pie-IX ♿ Good 💷 Moderate

ÉCOMUSÉE DU FIER MONDE

www.ecomusee.qc.ca

Photographs and period objects illustrate the Industrial Revolution and its impact on Montréal and its people.

➕ E8 ✉ 2050 rue Amherst ☎ 514/528-8444 🕐 Wed 11–8, Thu, Fri 9.30–4, Sat, Sun 10.30–5 🚇 Berri-UQAM 🚌 14, 15, 125 ♿ Good 💷 Moderate

MAISONNEUVE

Maisonneuve began as a model city, created by French-speaking citizens who felt they would be better off separated from the then predominantly Anglo-Saxon city of Montréal. For 35 years from 1883 it enjoyed its status as a self-contained city, as the ruling elite commissioned wide boulevards and fine public buildings, many of them designed by Marius Dufresne. Seek out the Fire Station (4300 rue Notre-Dame Est), which owes a considerable architectural debt to Frank Lloyd Wright, the Beaux-Arts Marché Maisonneuve (▷ 94) and the former public baths just

A Beaux-Arts delight, Château Dufresne is just as sumptuous inside

opposite. Also eye-catching are the Théâtre Denise Pelletier, near the junction of rue Morgan and rue Sainte-Catherine Est, and the Église Très-Saint-Nom-de-Jésus.

➕ H2 🚇 Pie-XI, Joliette, Viau

MARCHÉ MAISONNEUVE

www.marchespublics-mtl.com

The original Marché Maisonneuve, a magnificent 1912 Beaux-Arts building, is now a cultural center, but farmers still sell their produce in the rather more modern building next door.

➕ H2 ✉ 4445 rue Ontario Est ☎ 514/937-7754 🕐 Mon–Wed, Sat 7–6, Thu, Fri 7am–8pm, Sun 7–5 🚇 Pie-XI, Viau

PARC MAISONNEUVE

Parc Maisonneuve's slopes and frozen lakes provide a great spot for tobogganing, cross-country skiing and skating in winter. In summer the park is ideal for picnics, walking, cycling, and you can even play golf.

➕ E1 ✉ 4601 rue Sherbrooke Est and boulevard Pie-XI ☎ 514/872-6555 🕐 Daily 6am–9pm 🚇 Viau, Pie-IX ♿ Good 🅿 Park free. Golf course/parking moderate

PLANETARIUM RIO TINTO ALCAN

espacepourlavie.ca/en/planetarium

Montréal's old planetarium closed and was replaced with this state-of-the-art creation in 2013, which forms part of the Olympic Park and Biodome-Insectarium-Jardin Botanique ensemble.

➕ G1 ✉ 4801 avenue Pierre-De-Coubertin ☎ 514/868-3000 or 514/872-4530 🕐 Sun–Wed 9–5, Thu–Sat 9–8 🚇 Viau 🚌 34, 125, 132 🅿 Expensive

LE VILLAGE

A few blocks from the Quartier Latin, the Village forms the heart of Montréal's vibrant gay and lesbian community. Known for its nightlife, the area is especially lively during the *Divers Cité* festival in August and Black & Blue festival in October.

➕ F8 ✉ rue Sainte-Catherine, roughly from St-Hubert to De Lorimier 🚇 Beaudry or Papineau

Cycling through Maisonneuve Park on a bicycle made for two

At the fringes of Montréal's down-town core, and at the heart of the Saint Lawrence River, are two islands and a variety of sights that are well worth making a special journey to visit.

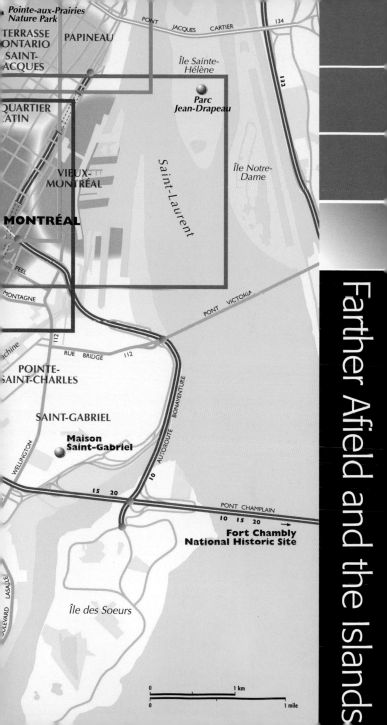

Pointe-aux-Prairies
Nature Park

TERRASSE
ONTARIO
SAINT-
JACQUES

PAPINEAU

PONT JACQUES CARTIER

134

132

Île Sainte-
Hélène

*Parc
Jean-Drapeau*

QUARTIER
LATIN

VIEUX-
MONTRÉAL

Saint-Laurent

Île Notre-
Dame

MONTRÉAL

PEEL

MONTAGNE

PONT VICTORIA

112

RUE BRIDGE 112

POINTE-
SAINT-CHARLES

SAINT-GABRIEL

AUTOROUTE BONAVENTURE

**Maison
Saint-Gabriel**

WELLINGTON

10

15 20

10 15 20

PONT CHAMPLAIN

**Fort Chambly
National Historic Site**

BOULEVARD LASALLE

Île des Soeurs

0   1 km

0   1 mile

Canal de Lachine and Marché Atwater

HIGHLIGHTS

● Guided tours of the canal
● Boating on the canal
● Cycling the canalside path
● Sampling the fare at the Atwater Market

TIP

● There are two best times to visit Marché Atwater: weekday mornings for hassle-free shopping; after-work hours and Saturdays for bustling people-watching.

Revitalized and reopened for public recreation, the former industrial canal offers historic sites, pleasant waterside walks and boating. The nearby Marché Atwater is full of enticing aromas and colorful food displays.

From industry to leisure When it opened in 1825, the Canal de Lachine bypassed the Lachine Rapids to provide a lifeline between the industries of Lachine and their world-wide trading partners. Later industrial decline, coupled with the opening of the Saint Lawrence Seaway, led to the canal becoming neglected, and it closed in 1970. Its historic importance was never forgotten, though, and a massive restoration project led to its reopening in 2002 as a National Historic Site of Canada. Locks were restored, the Peel basin was

Clockwise from left: on a bicycle path at Lachine Canal; Marché Atwater sells a wide range of fresh foods; a nursery at Marché Atwater catches the attention of a cyclist; patisserie on sale at the market; Lachine National Historic Site

dredged, bridges were renovated and a Visitor Service Centre built. Now pleasure craft and cruise boats dot the water in summer, and its 11km (7 miles) are lined by pedestrian and cycle paths and grassy picnic places. There is also an interesting exhibition about the history of the fur trade.

Atwater You can't miss the Marché Atwater, a monumental art deco building with a tall clock tower, particularly during summer when the stands spill outside. With two floors undercover, it has a magnificent array of quality foods, including deli goods, fish and sushi, gourmet foods, cheese specialists, butchers, bakers, a beer store, and beautifully displayed fresh fruit, vegetables and flowers. If you want to shop for the finest local and organic produce, or hard-to-find imported specialties, this is your place.

THE BASICS

Lachine Canal National Historic Site

www.pc.gc.ca/lhn-nhs/qc/canallachine

✛ F14/C17

✉ From Vieux Port to Lachine

☎ 514/283-6054

🕐 Daily sunrise–11pm. Fur Trade Museum: mid-Jun to Sep 1 daily 10–5

🚇 Lionel-Groulx, Charlevoix

🚌 57, 61, 78, 107, 195

💷 Canal: free; parking inexpensive

❓ Guided tours

Atwater Market

www.marchespublics-mtl.com

✛ D16

✉ 138 Avenue Atwater

☎ 514/937-7754;

🕐 Mon–Wed 7–6, Thu 7–7, Fri 7am–8pm, Sat–Sun 7–5

🚇 Lionel-Groulx

🚌 78, 195

Petite Italie

Shop for local ingredients and eat at one of the district's trattorias

HIGHLIGHTS

● Semaine Italienne
● Madonna della Defesa Church
● Dante Park
● Marché Jean-Talon

Trattorias, ristorantes and caffès; gelati, espresso and pasta; a park and street named after Dante; and a fine Romanesque church—there's little doubt that this is Montréal's Italian quarter.

From the old country There have been two main waves of Italian immigration into Montréal—the first toward the end of the 19th century, and again after World War II, and though the area is now home to a more eclectic mix, it is still the Italian flavor that predominates.

Cultural treasures Thanks to its distance from downtown, the character of Little Italy has remained relatively intact. Shopping is a major attraction: Explore its section of boulevard Saint-Laurent and rue Dante, which form the commercial hub for Italian fashion and footwear designs, restaurants and cafés; or head for the Marché Jean-Talon for fresh ingredients and gourmet foods. Be sure to allow time to visit the splendid Madonna della Defesa Church on avenue Henri-Julien, a fine Romanesque building containing a Carrera marble altar and remarkable frescoes by Guido Nincheri (1885–1973). Dante Park, next to the church, is a great place for relaxing and people-watching, and the Casa d'Italia is the local community center.

Festival time Each August the Semaine Italienne (Italian Week; www.italianweek.ca) celebrates Montréal's Italian community with music, dance, theater and, of course, food and drink. The rest of the time, there's nothing better than a spot of window-shopping.

THE BASICS

✚ Off map at A5
✉ Between rues Saint-Zotique, Drolet, Jean-Talon and avenue du Parc
🚇 Jean-Talon
🚌 30, 55

Marché Jean-Talon
www.marchespublics-mtl.com
✉ 7070 rue Henri-Julien ☎ 514/937-7754
🕐 Mon–Wed 7–6, Thu, Fri 7am–8pm, Sat 7–6, Sun 7–5
🚇 Jean-Talon

Parc Jean-Drapeau

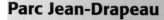

HIGHLIGHTS

- La Biosphère
- La Ronde amusement park
- Musée Stewart
- Public art
- The beach

TIPS

- You can save waiting time for rides at La Ronde with the Flash Pass reservation system.
- The dress code at the casino is not too strict (except for Nuances restaurant), but is worth checking out before a visit. The minimum age is 18.

Two islands in the Saint Lawrence River provide a vast playground close to downtown, offering theme park rides, motor racing, concerts, gambling, a historic site and an environmental museum.

La Biosphère When Expo '67 opened, the US Pavilion was then the world's largest geodesic dome. It went on to become the world's largest aviary, but after fire destroyed its acrylic skin in 1976 the metal skeleton was all that survived. Today this great transparent golf ball encloses a fascinating environmental museum, run by the government agency Environment Canada. In addition to the exhibits and multimedia activities, there are guided tours to explain the building's wind turbine and geothermal power systems and its wastewater treatment wetlands.

Clockwise from top left: Formula 1 Grand Prix race at the Gilles-Villeneuve circuit; La Biosphère; entrance to La Ronde amusement park; the casino; Alexander Calder's sculpture, Man, on Île Sainte-Hélène; La Ronde

THE BASICS

www.parcjeandrapeau.com
J6–11 and off map ✉ Société du parc Jean-Drapeau, 1 circuit Gilles-Villeneuve
☎ 514/872- 6120
🕐 Daily 6am–midnight
🍴 Restaurants and snack bars on both islands
Ⓜ Jean-Drapeau
🚌 167 (year-round), 169 (seasonal) 🚢 Jacques-Cartier Pier 🎫 Free; beach moderate; parking inexpensive

La Biosphère
http://biosphere.ec.gc.ca
✉ 160 Chemin Tour-de-l'Isle, Île Sainte-Hélène
☎ 514/283-5000
🕐 Jun– Sep daily 10–5; Oct–May Wed–Sun 10–5
🎫 Moderate

La Ronde
www.laronde.com
✉ 22 Chemin Macdonald, Île Sainte-Hélène
☎ 514/397-2000
🕐 Mid-May to early Sep daily from 10am; Sep daily from noon; Oct Sat–Sun from noon. Closing varies seasonally 🎫 Expensive

Musée Stewart
www.stewart-museum.org
✉ Île Sainte-Hélène
☎ 514/861-6701
🕐 Wed–Sun 11–5
🎫 Moderate

Casino de Montréal
www.casinosduquebec.com
✉ Île Notre-Dame ☎ 514/392-2746 🕐 Daily 24 hours
Ⓜ Jean-Drapeau 🚌 167

Île Notre-Dame When the Métro system was being excavated in the 1960s, they needed somewhere to deposit all the waste, and the then mayor, Jean Drapeau, came up with the scheme to create an island to host the upcoming world fair. Former pavilions from the fair house a casino, the Gilles-Villeneuve motor-racing circuit hosts the Canadian Grand Prix, an artificial lakeside beach is a huge attraction, and there's a vast floral park, laced with canals and waterways, built in 1980.

Île Saint-Hélène Île Saint-Hélène was linked to the city when the Jacques Cartier bridge was built in 1930, then doubled in size (more Métro rubble) for Expo '67. Now it is best known for the La Ronde amusement park, for open-air concerts and for the summer fireworks competitions. There is also the Musée Stewart history museum.

More to See

COSMODÔME

www.cosmodome.org

The adventure of space exploration is the focus here. Exhibits include replicas of rockets and space ships, films, games and demonstrations. ✚ Off map ✉ 2150 autoroute de Laurentides, Laval ☎ 514/978-3600 or 800/565-2267 ◷ Late Jun to mid-Sep daily 10–5; mid-Sep to late Jun Tue–Sun 10–5 Ⓜ Montmorency, then bus 61 Ⓦ Expensive

FORT CHAMBLY NATIONAL HISTORIC SITE

www.pc.gc.ca

Standing beside the Richelieu River, close to where it tumbles over the Chambly rapids, this great square bastion was built by the French in the early 18th century to replace a wooden fort. The British took it over, after their conquest of "New France", and stood guard here as American forces threatened, first during their Revolutionary War and then in the war of 1812. Happily, the fort survived and was restored during the 1980s. Today, it again reflects its ori-gins, with exhibitions about the life of the early French settlers. Guides are on hand to discuss the history of the fort. There are also colorful special events, with costumed reenactments. ✚ Off map ✉ 2 rue de Richelieu, Chambly ☎ 450/658-1585, 888/773-8888 ◷ Mid-May to late Jun and early Sep to late Oct Wed–Sun 10–5; late Jun to Aug daily 10–6 🚆 Chambly-Richelieu-Carignan from downtown Ⓦ Moderate

MAISON SAINT-GABRIEL

www.maisonsaint-gabriel.qc.ca

St. Marguerite Bourgeoys ran a farm and school from this 17th-century house among Pointe-Saint-Charles tenements. In addition to special exhibitions, the house has some 15,000 objects from the 17th century onward, including furniture, art and craft works, tools and artifacts, clothing, silverware and documents. ✚ F16 ✉ 2146 place Dublin ☎ 514/935-8136 ◷ Late Jun to early Sep Tue–Sun 11–6; mid-Apr to late Jun, early Sep to mid-Dec Tue–Sun 1–5 Ⓜ Charlevoix 🚌 57, 61 ♿ Good Ⓦ Moderate

Maison Saint-Gabriel, dating back to 1668, is now a heritage museum

POINTE-AUX-PRAIRIES NATURE PARK

ville.montreal.qc.ca

This park sits at the northeastern tip of Montréal island, where the Saint Lawrence river meets the Rivière des Prairies, and covers 261ha (645 acres) of forest, pastures and marshland. Special pathways have been set out for birding, and activities range from cycling and rollerblading in summer to cross-country skiing and tobogganing in winter.

🗺 Off map ✉ 14905 rue Sherbrooke Est ☎ 514/280-6691 🕐 Park: daily dawn–dusk; Heritage Centre: late Apr to late Oct daily 9.30–4.30; Nature Interpretation Centre: late Apr to mid-Sep Wed–Mon 9.30 4.30 🚇 Honoré-Meaugrand, then bus 186 🍴 Snack bar 💵 Free; parking inexpensive

TOHU

www.tohu.ca

This round building out in the Complexe Environnemental de Saint-Michel is a center for the circus arts and incorporates an exciting performance space and exhibitions.

🗺 Off map at A3 ✉ 2345 rue Jarry Est ☎ 514/376-8648 🕐 Box office daily 9–5 🚇 Jarry, then bus 193 east; Iberville, then bus 94 north 🚌 57, 61 ♿ Very good

WESTMOUNT

www.westmount.org

On the western slopes of Mont-Royal is Westmount, with a mix of fine old English-style mansions, parks, specialty shopping and modern architecture, of which Westmount Square—a black metal and tinted-glass building by Mies van der Rohe—is the showpiece. In Parc Westmount, older buildings are the 1899 Victoria Hall, now a community center, and the 1927 Conservatory, which produces plants for the city and contains a totem pole from British Columbia. The surrounding park has a shady waterway and a swimming pool.

🗺 B15 🚇 Vendôme, Atwater 🚌 24, 37, 63, 66, 90, 104, 124, 138

Victoria Hall Gallery and Conservatory

✉ 4626 rue Sherbrooke Ouest ☎ 514/989-5353 🕐 Conservatory: Mon–Fri 10–2.30, Sat, Sun 10–4.45 💵 Free

Westmount Square, a striking building by Mies van der Rohe

Restaurants

PRICES

Prices are approximate, based on a 3-course meal for one person.

$$$	over $40
$$	$20–$40
$	under $20

JOE BEEF ($$)
www.joebeef.com
Joe Beef is named for a tavern-keeper who was the hero of this formerly blue-collar neighborhood. The atmosphere is old-time and the beef is big-time.
🚩 D15 ✉ 2491 rue Notre-Dame Ouest ☎ 514/935-6504 🕓 Tue–Sat dinner 🚇 Lionel-Groulx

LIMON ($$)
www.limon.ca
This is an upscale spot for updated Mexican cuisine, such as fried calamari in chipotle sauce and lime tart finished with tequila cream.
🚩 D15 ✉ 2472 rue Notre-Dame Ouest ☎ 514/509-1237 🕓 Mon–Fri 11–11, Sat–Sun 5–11 🚇 Lionel-Groulx

LIVERPOOL HOUSE ($$)
www.joebeef.com
The oyster bar is the draw to this seafood sibling of the famed Joe Beef. Oysters, shrimp, scallops and more.
🚩 D15 ✉ 2501 rue Notre-Dame Ouest ☎ 514/313-6049 🕓 Tue–Sat dinner 🚇 Lionel-Groulx

PASTICCERIA ALATI-CASERTA ($)
www.alaticaserta.com
No place to sit, but just join the people on the street outside, all munching on the best *cannoli* (a sweet pastry) in town. Everything, from the dough to the frosting, is done in-house.
🚩 Off map ✉ 277 rue Dante ☎ 514/271-3013 🕓 Mon 10–5, Tue, Wed 8–6, Thu 8–7, Fri 8–7.30, Sat 8–5.30, Sun 9–5 🚇 Jean-Talon

PIZZERIA GEPPETTO ($)
www.geppettopizza.com
This little Italian spot serves pizzas beyond the usual—try mushroom with chèvre and truffle oil, and finish off with the *gelato* of the day.
🚩 D15 ✉ 2504 rue Notre-Dame Ouest ☎ 514/903-3737 🕓 Mon–Wed 12–10, Thu, Fri 12–12, Sat 5–12, Sun 5–10 🚇 Lionel-Groulx

RESTAURANT ROW

The stretch of rue Notre-Dame between Atwater and rue Guy is the city's latest dining hot spot, becoming popular with the refurbishing of the Theatre Corona, at its heart. Restaurants surrounding the theater include everything from local cuisine to updated Mexican. Expect the scene to continue to change and grow.

PIZZERIA NAPOLETANA ($–$$)
www.napoletana.com
Bring your own wine (big carafes of cold water are free) to this crowded, friendly spot, famed for thin-crust pizza and pasta dishes. It offers 41 different types of pizza and 34 pasta options.
🚩 Off map ✉ 189 rue Dante ☎ 514/276-8226 🕓 Mon–Thu 11–11, Fri–Sat 11am–midnight, Sun 12–11 🚇 De Castelneau

PREMIÈRE MOISSON ($)
www.premieremoisson.com
At the canal end of the Atwater Market, this is the place for flaky croissants and *café au lait* in a bowl. Or sample *cretons* (a pork spread) on a fresh-baked baguette. There is a branch at the Jean-Talon Market and other outlets around the city.
🚩 D16 ✉ Atwater Market, 138 ave Atwater ☎ 514/932-0328 🕓 Mon–Wed 7–6, Thu 7–7, Fri 7am–8pm, Sat–Sun 7–5 🚇 Lionel-Groulx

QUOI DE N'OEUFS ($)
Enjoy great Eggs Benedict and other creative egg dishes for brunch while shopping at Atwater Market. Also crêpes and French toast. There may be a line, but it moves fast.
🚩 D15 ✉ 2745 rue Notre-Dame Ouest ☎ 514/931-3999 🕓 Mon–Sat 7–3, Sun 8–3 🚇 Lionel-Groulx

Whether you like to stay in the thick of it or opt for some peace and quiet, or prefer large chain hotels rather than a more intimate establishment, Montréal can satisfy all tastes.

Introduction

Montréal has a wide range of high-quality accommodations, from boutique hotels in the old port area to glittering luxury places in the downtown and Mont-Royal districts.

Where to Stay

The most charming area to stay is Vieux-Montréal, where around a dozen intimate and interesting hotels in the mid- and luxury ranges offer accommodations close to the city's main historic sights. If you prefer to be nearer to the best shopping, or want a larger, international or chain hotel, then the best bet is downtown, which is still convenient for sightseeing. Budget hotels are relatively thin on the ground, except in the Quartier Latin and around, though here the location, while good for nightlife and dining options, is far less appealing. Places near the bus station, in particular, are best avoided.

Best to Book

Although Montreál has plenty of accommodations, with more hotels opening every year, the city's increasing popularity with visitors means that it can still be difficult to secure a place to stay in high season and other busy times. Always book well ahead if you plan to visit from May to September, in the busy shopping weeks before Christmas, or during popular events. Try contacting the visitor center for last-minute and other options. Or consider staying in one of the city's many bed-and-breakfasts, though these can be some way from the city hub.

SAVING MONEY

Smaller hotels often have a variety of rooms at different prices, so don't assume the first room you are offered is the cheapest. Hotels that cater predominantly to business people often offer discounted weekend rates. Many hotels also offer discounted rates online and for longer stays. Tourisme Montréal has a year-round Sweet Deals promotion offering discounted hotel rooms (www.tourisme-montreal.org/Offers). Always ask what is included in a rate, especially regarding breakfasts.

Budget Hote

PRICES

Expect to pay up to $120 for a budget hotel

ANNE MA SOEUR ANNE

www.annemasoeuranne.com
Good-value hotel in the upscale Plateau district. Excellent in-room facilities, including high-speed wireless internet, voice mail, microwave, toaster-oven and coffee-maker. Continental breakfast is included.

➕ D8 ✉ 4119 rue Saint-Denis ☎ 514/281-3187, 877/281-3187 Ⓜ Mont-Royal, Sherbrooke

AUBERGE DE JEUNESSE YOUTH HOSTEL

www.hostellingmontreal.com
Superior hostel with 15 private rooms and 243 dormitory-style beds. Free WiFi.

➕ D13 ✉ 1030 rue Mackay ☎ 514/843-3317 or 866/843-3317 Ⓜ Lucien l'Allier

AUBERGE YWCA

www.ydesfemmesmtl.org
Simple rooms (63) for single, double and multiple occupancy. Women have access to YWCA health facilities.

➕ D13 ✉ 1355 boulevard René-Lévesque Ouest ☎ 514/866-9942 Ⓜ Lucien L'Allier

BIENVENUE B&B

www.bienvenuebb.com
Cozy bed-and-breakfast on a pleasant residential street of old stone houses, close to the buzzing rue Saint-Denis and boulevard Saint-Laurent. The 12 rooms are individually styled and some have private bathrooms.

➕ D9 ✉ 3950 avenue Laval ☎ 514/844-5897 or 800/227-5897 Ⓜ Sherbrooke

HÔTEL LE ROBERVAL

www.leroberval.com
No-frills hotel with 76 rooms and suites near downtown.

➕ F9 ✉ 505 boulevard René-Lévesque Est ☎ 514/286-5215 Ⓜ Champ-de-Mars, Berri-UQAM

HÔTEL LE ST-ANDRÉ

www.hotelsaintandre.ca
Charming 62-room hotel close to Vieux-Montréal and the Quartier Latin.

➕ F9 ✉ 1285 rue Saint-André ☎ 514/849-7070 or 800/265-7071 Ⓜ Berri-UQAM

BED-AND-BREAKFAST

B&B options can be booked through tourist offices and at www.tourisme-montreal.org, the city's official tourism site, which has numerous and regularly updated deals across all price ranges, along with a useful neighborhood search option.

Good websites for bed-and-breakfast in Montréal include www.bedandbreakfast.com and www.canadian bandbguide.ca.

HOTEL LE SAINT-MALO

www.hotel-saint-malo.com
A stylish hotel close to the best part of rue Sainte-Catherine. All rooms have individual temperature control, air conditioning, high-speed internet, cable TV and private bathroom.

➕ C13 ✉ 1455 rue du Fort ☎ 514/931-7366 Ⓜ Guy-Concordia

HOTEL STAY CENTRE VILLE

http://hotelstaycentreville.ca
Reasonably priced rooms in a renovated 1916 commercial building, in a downtown location. Each of the 13 rooms is different, but all have air conditioning, flat-screen TV and WiFi.

➕ F9 ✉ 505 boulevard de Maisonneuve Est ☎ 514/303-7584 Ⓜ Berri-UQAM

MCGILL UNIVERSITY

www.mcgill.ca/residences/summer
During the summer recess (mid-May to Aug), visitors can rent student lodgings at McGill University—more than 1,000 rooms. These are inexpensive, in the city center, in a pleasant campus setting and include use of the university gym, pool and other facilities. Some rooms have access to kitchenettes, but most have shared bathroom facilities.

➕ D11 ✉ 3935 rue University ☎ 514/398-5200 or 3471 (new Residence Hall) Ⓜ McGill

WHERE TO STAY BUDGET HOTELS

109

Expect to pay between $120 and $250 for a mid-range hotel

AUBERGE BONAPARTE

www.bonaparte.com
This delightful 31-room inn, in the heart of Vieux-Montréal, has views of the gardens of the Basilique Notre-Dame, which are right next door.
✚ F11 ✉ 447 rue Saint-François-Xavier ☎ 514/844-1448 🚇 Place d'Armes

AUBERGE LES BONS MATINS

www.bonsmatins.com
Cozy century-old B&B in a leafy downtown cul-de-sac, with some stunning features and wonderful breakfasts.
✚ D13 ✉ 1401 avenue Argyle ☎ 514/931-9167 🚇 Lucien L'Allier

AUBERGE DE LA FONTAINE

www.aubergedelafontaine.com
With just 18 rooms and three suites, this intimate hotel, near a bicycle path, faces Parc Lafontaine in the trendy Plateau Mont-Royal district. It is a welcoming little inn with some vivid but appealing decoration and a good breakfast included in the room rate.
✚ D7 ✉ 1301 rue Rachel Est ☎ 514/597-0166 or 800/597-0597 🚇 Mont-Royal

AUBERGE LE JARDIN D'ANTOINE

www.aubergejardinantoine.com
Reproduction antiques lend a charming period feel to this 25-room hotel, which sits at the heart of the rue Saint-Denis and Quartier Latin nightlife and entertainment district.
✚ E9 ✉ 2024 rue Saint-Denis ☎ 514/843-4506 or 800/361-4506 🚇 Berri-UQAM

AUBERGE DE LA PLACE ROYALE

www.aubergedelaplaceroyale.com
A superior B&B in a fine 19th-century Vieux-Port building, with nine moderate rooms and three suites. It's filled with antiques, and there are views of the waterfront from the most expensive rooms. The other rooms look onto a back street.
✚ G11 ✉ 115 rue de la Commune Ouest ☎ 514/281-0938 🚇 Place-d'Armes

RESERVATIONS

Although greater Montréal has some 23,000 hotel beds, advance reservations are advisable, particularly from May to September. Even if you guarantee your booking with a credit card, reconfirm a few days ahead. Receptionists are usually bilingual in French and English. If you arrive without accommodations, the city's tourist offices will help you to find a room.

BEST WESTERN EUROPA CENTRE-VILLE

www.hoteleuropa.com
The excellent downtown location and good selection of restaurants here distinguish this 184-room hotel.
✚ D12 ✉ 1240 rue Drummond ☎ 514/866-6492 or 800/361-3000 🚇 Peel, Guy-Concordia

CHÂTEAU VERSAILLES

www.chateauversaillesmontreal.com
This has become one of the city's most elegant hotels, with 65 rooms and suites. Many rooms have fireplaces.
✚ C13 ✉ 1659 rue Sherbrooke Ouest ☎ 514/933-8111 or 888/933-8111 🚇 Guy-Concordia

GARDEN INN CENTRE-VILLE

www.hiltongardenmontreal.com
The location, steps from the Underground City and the cultural center of place des Arts, couldn't be better. The contemporary hotel offers underground parking, a sauna, whirlpool, fitness room and indoor rooftop pool.
✚ D10 ✉ 380 rue Sherbrooke Ouest ☎ 514/840-0010 🚇 Place-des-Arts

HÔTEL ARMOR MANOIR SHERBROOKE

www.armormanoir.com
Converted Victorian building with 22 pleasant

rooms. A continental breakfast is included.
⊞ E9 ✉ 157 rue Sherbrooke Est ☎ 514/845-0915 or 800/203-5485 Ⓜ Sherbrooke

HÔTEL DE L'INSTITUT
www.ithq.qc.ca
Top civil servants love this 42-room hotel on the top floors of Québec's best hotel training school, right in the Quartier Latin.
⊞ E9 ✉ 3535 rue Saint-Denis ☎ 514/282-5120 or 800/361-5111 Ⓜ Sherbrooke

HÔTEL LORD BERRI
www.lordberri.com
Good modern hotel with 154 rooms near the Université du Québec à Montréal and rue Saint-Denis.
⊞ F19 ✉ 1199 rue Berri ☎ 514/845-9236 or 888/363-0363 Ⓜ Berri-UQAM

HÔTEL MARITIME PLAZA
www.tidanhotels.com
A favorite with bus tours, this hotel is convenient for shops and museums. There are 214 rooms and suites.
⊞ D13 ✉ 1155 rue Guy ☎ 514/932-1411 or 800/363-6255 Ⓜ Guy-Concordia, Lucien L'Allier

LOEWS HÔTEL VOGUE
www.loewshotels.com
The 142 rooms and suites of this fashionable downtown hotel all have whirlpool baths, televisions and phones.
⊞ D12 ✉ 1425 rue de la Montagne ☎ 514/285-5555 or 800/465-6654 Ⓜ Peel, Guy-Concordia

LE NOUVEL HÔTEL
www.lenouvelhotel.com
This modern, functional hotel, with 175 rooms, is in a convenient location.
⊞ D13 ✉ 1740 boulevard René-Lévesque Ouest ☎ 514/931-8841 or 800/363-6063 Ⓜ Guy-Concordia

LE PETIT HOTEL
www.petithotelmontreal.com
This 24-room hotel, close to Vieux Montréal and the waterfront, has wired and wireless internet, and massage jet showers. Breakfast and local telephone calls are included.
⊞ F11 ✉ 168 rue Saint-Paul Ouest ☎ 514/940-0360, 877/530-0360 Ⓜ Place-d'Armes

---

HIDDEN COSTS
To avoid any nasty shocks on checking out of your hotel, it is worth knowing the various taxes and other hidden charges that will appear on Montréal bills. Some hotels will include these charges in the published room rate: Most will not. The additions include the country-wide Goods and Services Tax (GST) at five percent and a provincial sales tax of 7.5 percent. There is also a city tax of three percent. Be aware that hotels will also often charge high rates for any direct-dial calls made from your room.

LE SAINT-SULPICE
www.lesaintsulpice.com
A good location—right by the Basilique Notre-Dame—is the main draw of this 108-room hotel, opened in 2002 in a modern building designed to blend with its period surroundings.
⊞ F11 ✉ 414 rue Saint-Sulpice ☎ 514/288-1000 or 877/785-7423 Ⓜ Place-d'Armes

SIR MONTCALM
www.sirmontcalm.com
In Le Village, this chic B&B is gay-owned and operated, but straight-friendly too. The contemporary decor is stunning and the price includes a four-course breakfast.
⊞ F9 ✉ 1453 Montcalm ☎ 514/522-7747 Ⓜ Beaudry

SOFITEL MONTRÉAL
www.sofitel.com
Modern skyscraper hotel with 241 bright, spacious rooms and stylish interiors.
⊞ D12 ✉ 1155 rue Sherbrooke Ouest ☎ 514/285-9000 or 877/285-9001 Ⓜ Peel

SQUARE PHILLIPS
www.squarephillips.com
This 10-floor historic building is now an apartment hotel. Its 160 studios and suites each have a kitchen, work space, free internet and two TVs, and the hotel has a pool, laundromat and fitness room.
⊞ E11 ✉ 1193 place Phillips ☎ 514/393-1193 or 866/393-1193 Ⓜ McGill

PRICES

Expect to pay over $250 for a luxury hotel

FAIRMONT LE REINE ELIZABETH

www.fairmont.com
This long-established hotel has more than 1,000 rooms and suites, and sits above the main railway station. It is the hotel in which John Lennon and Yoko staged their famous "bed-in" in 1969. Excellent modern rooms and service, especially on the "Gold Floor." ✚ E12 ✉ 900 boulevard René-Lévesque Ouest ☎ 514/861-3511 or 866/540-4483 🚇 Bonaventure

HÔTEL (10)

www.hotel10montreal.com
One of the city's most striking hotels, starkly contemporary in design and convenient for Quartier Latin nightlife. 136 rooms and 12 suites. ✚ E10 ✉ 10 rue Sherbrooke Ouest ☎ 514/843-6000 or 855/390-6787 🚇 Saint-Laurent

HÔTEL NELLIGAN

www.hotelnelligan.com
A beautiful, romantic hotel in an 1850s building, with 35 rooms and 28 suites. In a perfect Vieux-Montréal spot near Basilique Notre-Dame. ✚ F11 ✉ 106 rue Saint-Paul Ouest ☎ 514/788-2040 or 877/788-2040 🚇 Place-d'Armes

HOTEL LE ST-JAMES

www.hotellestjames.com
Built in 1870, this grand building is supremely luxurious in the classic style of its era, with an elegant sweeping staircase leading from a lofty entrance hall. The rooms and suites are spacious (the best cost $2,500–$3,500 a night), and there's fine dining and a spa—and a luxury yacht for guests' use. Close to the Convention Centre and World Trade Centre. ✚ F11 ✉ 355 rue St-Jacques ☎ 514/841-3111 or 866/841-3111 🚇 Square-Victoria, Place d'Armes

HÔTEL ST-PAUL

www.hotelstpaul.com
Choose between airy white "sky rooms," with large windows, and "earth rooms" in warmer

CHILDREN

Some hotels have family-plan deals that allow children sharing a room with their parents to stay (and sometimes eat) free. Most have rooms equipped with two double beds and some provide a third, smaller bed in the same room for a modest fee. More expensive hotels may offer child-minding services and children's programs. Swimming pools and in-room electronic games and movies also make some hotels particularly child-friendly.

shades at this designer boutique hotel on the southern edge of Vieux-Montréal. Also known for its celebrated Cube restaurant. 96 rooms and 24 suites. ✚ F12 ✉ 355 rue McGill ☎ 514/380-2222 or 866/380-2202 🚇 Square-Victoria

MONTRÉAL AIRPORT MARRIOTT HOTEL

www.marriott.com
This striking new hotel is connected directly to the Pierre-Trudeau Airport in Dorval, with easy access to the city. All 272 rooms and 7 suites have high-speed internet, flat-screen TVs and chic decor. ✚ Off map ✉ 800 place Leigh-Capreol, Dorval ☎ 514/636-6700, 866/580-6279 🚇 Aérobus from central bus station at Berri-UQAM

PIERRE-DU-CALVET

www.pierreducalvet.ca
In an 18th-century building in Vieux-Montréal with nine sumptuously decorated rooms. Fine restaurant. ✚ G10 ✉ 405 rue Bonsecours ☎ 514/282-1725 or 866/544-1725 🚇 Champ-de-Mars

W MONTRÉAL

www.wmontrealhotel.com
Chic, modern design, Bliss spas and a "whatever, whenever" approach to service. 152 rooms and 30 suites. ✚ E12 ✉ 901 Square-Victoria ☎ 514/395-3100 or 888/627-7081 🚇 Square-Victoria

Need to Know

Here is key information to help smooth your path both before you go and when you arrive. Get savvy with the local transportation, explore the Montréal websites or check out what festivals are taking place.

Planning Ahead

When to Go

The best time to visit Montréal is between late May and late October. The summer, from the end of June to the first weekend in September, is rich in festivals. Fall brings cooler weather, better for walking; the parks can be spectacular. In winter, a visit can be coupled with a trip to a ski resort.

AVERAGE DAILY MAXIMUM TEMPERATURES

	JAN	FEB	MAR	APR	MAY	JUN	JUL	AUG	SEP	OCT	NOV	DEC
°F	18°F	20°F	31°F	45°F	63°F	73°F	79°F	77°F	69°F	56°F	43°F	33°F
°C	-8°C	-7°C	-1°C	7°C	17°C	23°C	26°C	25°C	21°C	13°C	6°C	1°C

Spring (April to May) The leap between winter and summer can be very abrupt. It is also the least attractive time of year as the melting snow reveals dead grass littered with the debris of winter.

Summer (June to August) begins on June 24, the date of the *Québec Fête National*. The city can be very hot and humid, especially in downtown.

Fall (September to October), with cooler temperatures and sunny days, makes for ideal exploring. There are fewer visitors, so you can see the city as the locals do.

Winter (November to March), Montréal's defining season, can be brutally cold, with occasional blizzards that shut down the city. There's often a brief thaw in January.

WHAT'S ON

January/February *Fête des Neiges*: Celebrations in Parc Jean-Drapeau.

February *Montréal High Lights Festival:* Celebrates winter with culinary and cultural events and lights.

March *St. Patrick's Day Parade*.

May *Festival Trans-Ameriques*: New drama.

June *Grand Prix du Canada*: Formula 1 on Île Notre-Dame.

Tour d'Île: 40,000 bicyclists try this 50km (31-mile) trek through the city streets.

Suoni Per il Popolo: North America's largest avant-garde music festival.

Fringe Festival: Theater, dance and music.

June–July *Montréal International Jazz Festival*: The largest celebration of jazz music in the world brings top names in jazz to perform in concerts, many of them free.

International Fireworks Competition: Saturdays (mid-June to mid-July).

July *Juste Pour Rire (Just for Laughs)*: The world's largest comedy festival.

Nuits d'Afrique: Traditional African music and festivities on boulevard Saint-Laurent.

Franco Folies: 1,000 musicians take part in a celebration of French songs and music.

August *Divers/Cité*: Five days of gay pride events.

Italian Week: A week of Italian music, theater, food and other fun.

Festival des Films du Monde: World film festival.

October *Festival du Nouveau Cinéma*: Independent and avant-garde films/videos.

Useful Websites

www.montrealplus.ca
This broad travel guide provides information about Montréal lodging, dining, shopping and entertainment.

www.vieux.montreal.qc.ca
A comprehensive guide to historic Vieux-Montréal. Includes live webcams, maps and historical information and tours.

www.montrealgazette.com
News and features from the *Montréal Gazette,* the city's daily newspaper.

www.tourisme-montreal.org
You can download maps, print itineraries and read up on attractions and coming events on this, the official tourist information website.

www.montrealjazzfest.com
Every year some 2,000 jazz musicians perform more than 500 shows in Montréal's largest festival, the *Festival International de Jazz de Montréal.* This site includes a venue map, ticket information and performer news.

www.hahaha.com
The Just for Laughs comedy festival propelled performers such as Jerry Seinfeld and Ray Romano to comedy stardom. The site has news of this year's festival and ticket information.

www.parcjeandrapeau.com
Information on tourist attractions and events in the Parc Jean-Drapeau; also maps and history.

http://restomontreal.ca
Narrow your search for the perfect meal by keyword or district on this funky restaurant site.

www.smartshoppingmontreal.com
Updated daily to bring the latest news on sales and special deals on everything from high fashion to a factory outlet for Kosher sweets.

PRIME TRAVEL SITES

www.fodors.com
A complete travel-planning site. You can research prices and weather; book air tickets, cars and rooms; ask questions (and get answers) from fellow travelers; and find links to other sites.

www.montreal.com
Exhaustive lists of what to do, and where to sleep and eat. You'll find information for all tastes, from tourist sights to local activities.

INTERNET CAFÉS

There are internet cafés at the main visitor center and railway and bus stations. A full list of internet cafés can be found at www.pagesjaunes.ca or www.yellowpages.ca

Atwater Library and Computer Centre
www.atwaterlibrary.ca
A center with PCs. No food.
🚇 E9 ✉ 1200 avenue Atwater ☎ 514/935-7344
🕐 Mon, Wed 10–8, Tue, Thu–Fri 10–6, Sat 10–5
✋ $4 per hour

FINDING TICKETS

La Vitrine (www.lavitrine.com) is the place to get tickets to all Montréal events, and the best place for last-minute tickets.

Getting There

FLYING TIMES

Airport gate to airport gate, Montréal is about an hour by air from New York City; two hours from Chicago; four hours 30 minutes from Dallas; six hours from Los Angeles; six hours from London; and 22 hours from Sydney.

ARRIVING BY CAR

Montréal is 47km (29 miles) from the US border, and is accessed from New York City on the New York State Thruway (I-87), which in Canada becomes Route 15. Or you can take US I-89 north until it becomes Route 133 that then becomes Highway 35, from which you turn onto Route 10, a road that leads straight to Montréal's downtown. Coming from Massachusetts, follow I-91, and then pick up Route 55 and Route 10 through the Eastern Townships area to Montréal. From Boston, take I-93, I-89 and Route 133. If coming from elsewhere in Canada, use the Trans-Canada Highway (Highway 1), which crosses the city as Route 40, then Route 25, before heading eastward as Route 20. The main roads from Toronto and Ottawa are Routes 401 and 417 respectively. Both converge west of Montréal, where you can pick up Routes 20 or 40.

AIRPORTS

Montréal-Trudeau Airport is 22.5km (14 miles) southwest of the city and handles all commercial flights. Aéroport de Mirabel is 56km (35 miles) northwest of the city and handles flights by private planes.

ARRIVING BY AIR

Montréal's main airport for international and domestic flights is the Aéroport International Pierre-Elliott-Trudeau de Montréal (✉ 975 boulevard Roméo-Vachon Nord, Dorval; ☎ 514/394-7377; flight information toll-free in Canada 800/465-1213; www.admtl.com). The airport is more commonly known as Montréal-Trudeau or by its previous name, Dorval. Its international code is YUL. Considerable expansion and modernization have created a new international arrivals area and Transborder Zone for visitors to and from the United States. Passengers heading for the United States clear US Customs in Montréal before boarding, instead of at their US destination.

FROM THE AÉROPORT MONTRÉAL-TRUDEAU

If you are on a tight budget, then it is possible to use public transportation to reach the city, though it can be a slow process. Allow 60–90 minutes. Use the dedicated 747 bus line (☎ 514/868-3737 or 514/786-4636, www.stm.info), which runs from the airport in front of the main terminal building to the main bus station (Station Centrale Berri ✉ 505 boulevard

de Maisonneuve). En route it stops at or close to many of the city's main downtown hotels and attractions. Services depart regularly 24 hours a day, seven days a week (usually every 10 minutes, half-hourly and hourly through the night). Tickets can be obtained from the airport, bus-station ticket kiosks, Métro stations or the Hilton

hotel downtown. The cost is $10, with reductions for senior citizens and children between 5 and 12. Children under 5 travel free. You will need the correct change to buy tickets on board the bus. The ticket is valid across the STM transit network for 24 hours.

Free minibus shuttles run from the bus station to around 40 downtown, Vieux-Montréal and Quartier-Latin hotels, but check to see if you wouldn't be better off disembarking from the 747 service earlier and walking directly to your hotel. Seats can be pre-booked by calling ☎ 514/631-1856.

Taxis charge a set fare of around $42 (plus tip) from the airport to central downtown locations, from the Vieux-Montréal district to near avenue Les Pins, between Atwater and Papineau.

ARRIVING BY TRAIN

Canadian trains run by VIA Rail (☎ 514/989-2626 or 888/842-7245 in Québec; www.viarail.ca) and US trains operated by Amtrak (☎ 800/872-7245; www.amtrak.com) all arrive at Montréal's main railway station, the Gare Centrale (Central Station), behind the Fairmont Le Reine Elizabeth hotel at 895 rue de la Gauchetière Ouest. The station is connected to the Underground City at several points, and to the Bonaventure Métro station.

ARRIVING BY BUS

Montréal's Station Centrale d'Autobus at 505 boulevard de Maisonneuve Est (☎ 514/842-2281, www.gamtl.com) has connections to the Berri-UQAM Métro station. It handles all Greyhound (www.greyhound.ca) and other long-distance bus services from Canadian and some US cities, including Orléans Express (www.orleansexpress.com), which covers most routes in Québec province. The quickest buses to Québec City and Ottawa take 2 hours 20 minutes. Buses from New York take 8 hours and 7 hours from Boston.

Getting Around

TRAVEL INSURANCE

Travel insurance, including coverage for medical costs, is strongly recommended. Check your insurance coverage and buy a supplementary policy as needed.

VISITORS WITH DISABILITIES

Montréal's Métro system is not adapted for wheelchairs. There are few elevators and the escalators are not always dependable, so deep stations such as Snowdon and Lucien-L'Allier are difficult for anyone with mobility problems. The new, low-slung buses are a little better. Passengers with a cane or crutches can embark with care. They also accept wheelchairs at the rear exit doors, but space is limited and the entrance tight. Most major attractions and hotels are much better, with ramps and elevators, and facilities to help hearing- and vision-impaired visitors. For additional information contact Kéroul ✉ 4545 avenue Pierre-De Coubertin, Box 1000, Branch M, Montréal, H1V 0B2 ☎ 514/252-3104; www.keroul.qc.ca.

Montréal has 192 bus routes and a Métro system with 68 stations and links to more than 32km (20 miles) of walkways in the Underground City (☎ 514/786-4636; www.stm.info). There are four color-coded lines (green, orange, blue and yellow). You can buy flat-fare one-way tickets that are valid for 2 hours, either as singles ($3) or a discounted two-trip ticket ($2.75 per trip) at Métro booths and some retail outlets, but not on buses. Tickets are good on both the Métro and the buses (exclusions include the 747 airport service), but if you have to change from one to the other, get a transfer from your bus driver or from the machine in the Métro station where your journey started. Ten-trip tickets are also available ($25.50). Weekly and monthly passes are available. Multi-day multi-ride Métro/bus passes are $18 for three days, $10 for one day. An unlimited travel evening ticket (6pm to 5am the next morning) is available for $5. Bus passengers with no ticket or pass must have the exact fare.

The orange and green lines operate Monday to Friday 5.30am–12.30am, Saturday 5.30am–1am, Sunday 5.30am–12.30am. The blue line runs daily between 5.30am and 12.15am. Most buses keep running until around 12.30am, when a night service takes over on limited routes. The yellow line runs 5.30am–1am Monday to Friday and Sunday, and 5.30am–1.30am on Saturday.

ROUTES AND TICKETS
● Contact STM (Société de Transport de Montréal) ✉ Mezzanine Level, Berri-UQAM Métro Station ☎ 514/786-4636; www.stm.info ⏰ Mon–Fri 8–6

MÉTRO AND BUS SERVICES
● Four key stations provide the main interchanges between lines: Berri-UQAM (orange, green and yellow lines); Lionel-Groulx (green and orange); Snowdon (blue and orange); Jean-Talon (blue and orange).

• A one-day or three-day pass allows you to travel at will on buses or Métro. For further information ☎ 514/786-4636. Both may be purchased from selected Métro stations, the tourist office or downtown hotels.

• Commuter train services are operated by AMT (Agence Métropolitaine de Transport) on five lines with a total of 45 stations. They go to Dorion-Rigaud in the west, Deux-Montagnes and Blainville-Saint-Jérôme, both to the north, Mont-Saint-Hilaire, across the river to the east, and Delson-Candiac, south across the river. Bear in mind that these services are limited to the hours immediately before and after normal business hours. For more information visit www.amt.qc.ca.

TAXIS

Taxis stand outside main hotels, near the train station and at major intersections, and can be hailed on the street.
Cab companies include:
• Co-op ☎ 514/636-6666, www.cooptaxi.com
• Diamond ☎ 514/273-6331, www.taxidiamond.com
• A 10–15 percent tip is normal.

CAR RENTAL

To rent a car in Montréal you must be 25 or over (21 if using a major credit card).
• Avis ✉ 1225 rue Metcalfe ☎ 514/866-2847 or 800/879-2847
• Budget ✉ 895 rue de la Gauchetière ☎ 514/866-7675
• Hertz Canada ✉ 1073 rue Drummond ☎ 514/938-1717 or 800/654-3131 (English), 800/263-0678 (French)
• Thrifty-Québec ✉ 159 rue Saint-Antoine Ouest ☎ 514/875-1100
• National ✉ 1200 rue Stanley ☎ 514/878-2771 or 800/227-7368

WATERWAY TRANSPORT

It's worth taking a boat just to see some of the city from the river. Navettes Maritimes du St-Laurent (☎ 514/281-8000 or 866/228 3200, www.navettesmaritimes.com) runs ferries from Jacques Cartier Pier in the Vieux-Port to the Réal Bouvier Marina in Longueuil. Boats leave hourly from Montréal: mid-May to mid-Jun and early Sep to early Oct Sat, Sun 9.35–6.35; mid-Jun to early Sep Mon–Thu 9.35–6.35, Sat–Sun 8.35–10.35. From Longueuil start and finish times are a half-hour later.

TOURIST OFFICE

Montréal's main tourist office is the:
Centre Infotouriste
www.bonjourquebec.com
✉ 1255 rue Peel, Bureau 100 ☎ 514/873-2015 or 877/266-5687 in Canada and the US ◷ Jun–Labor Day daily 7am–8pm; Labor Day–May daily 9–6 Ⓟ Peel

Essential Facts

VISA AND PASSPORT INFORMATION

Check visa/passport requirements before leaving home:
www.gov.uk
www.cic.gc.ca

MONEY

Canadian dollars are the local currency, although US dollars are widely accepted. ATM cards are also widely accepted. French speakers sometimes call a penny a "sou," the nickel "cinq sous" and the quarter "vingt-cinq sous." English speakers call the dollar coin a "looney" after the bird (a loon) on its obverse and the bimetal $2 coin a "tooney."

ELECTRICITY

● Current in Canada is 110 volts AC (60Hz). Plug adaptors are needed to match the two-prong sockets.

MAIL

● You can find the location of main and smaller post offices at www.canadapost.ca
● Smaller post offices are inside shops, department stores and train stations wherever there are Postes Canada signs.
● Buy stamps from post offices, the Centre Infotouriste in rue Peel, train stations and bus terminals, the airport and stores.
● Within Canada, postcards and letters up to 30g are 63¢; 30–50g $1.10, over 50g $1.34. Cards and letters to the US cost $1.10 up to 30g. Rates for other destinations are $1.85 up to 30g and $2.68 from 30 to 50g.
● Letters sent for collection in hotels should be marked "Guest Mail, Hold for Arrival."

OPENING HOURS

● Shops: Mon–Fri 9 or 9.30–6, Sat 9–5. Some open Sun 12–5. Some stores open Thu, Fri 10–9, Sat 10–6, Sun 12–5.
● Banks: Mon–Fri 9–4. Some larger banks open Sat morning.
● Post offices: Mon–Fri 8.30–5.30. Some open Sat mornings.
● Restaurants: hours vary, but many of the city's eating places may only open for lunch Mon–Fri and only offer dinner on Sat, or limited other evenings during the week, usually from Thu. Some restaurants may close Sun and Mon.

PUBLIC HOLIDAYS

● January 1; Good Friday; Easter Monday; Victoria Day (3rd Mon in May); *Fête Nationale* (June 24); Canada Day (July 1); Labor Day (1st Mon in Sep); Thanksgiving (second Mon in Oct); December 25. Remembrance Day (Nov 11) is also widely observed.

SALES TAX

● Taxes are generally added to the displayed prices of goods in the stores, hotel rates, restaurant checks, car rental, etc, so you need to do a bit of mental arithmetic before deciding whether or not you have found a bargain. When tipping in a restaurant, you calculate the amount on the pre-tax total.

● There are two levels of sales tax: the federal Goods and Services Tax (GST), which is currently 5 percent; and the Québec provincial tax (TVQ or QST) of 9.975 percent. Hotel guests are also charged 3 percent tax per night.

● Tax refunds are no longer offered to visitors to Canada.

TELEPHONES

● Local calls from phone booths cost 50¢. This includes calls to all numbers in the 514 and 438 area codes—all municipalities on the island of Montréal itself—and to some numbers in the surrounding 450 area code (in off-island suburbs, Laval, Longueuil and Brossard).

● For a number outside the area you are in, dial 1, then the area code.

● For international and long-distance calls, buy a phone card, or find public phones that accept credit cards.

● Direct dial phones are common in many hotels and motels. A surcharge is levied, but some offer free local calls.

● Many organizations have toll-free numbers—800, 866, 888 or 877 prefix. Some operate within a province, others in Canada, and a few across North America. Dial 1 before the number.

● Information for local numbers can be reached by dialing 411.

● To call the US from Canada dial the area code and the number. To call the UK from Canada dial 011 44, followed by the area code (minus its first zero), and the number required.

● To call Canada from the US dial 1, the area code, and then the number. To call Canada from the UK dial 001, then the area code, and then the number.

USEFUL NUMBERS

American Express
☎ 800/869-3016; www.americanexpress.com
MasterCard ☎ 800/307-7309; www.mastercard.com
Visa ☎ 800/847-2911; . www.visa.com
Road breakdown
☎ 800/222-4357 or 514/861-1313

EMERGENCY NUMBERS

Police, fire, ambulance
☎ 911 or dial 0.
Lost and found:
bus or Métro ✉ Mezzanine Level, Berri-UQAM Métro ☎ 514/786-4636 🕐 Mon–Fri 8–6; for taxis contact the cab company concerned. Elsewhere contact the MUC Police (www.spvm.wc.ca)
US Consulate ✉ 1155 rue Saint-Alexandre
☎ 514/398-9695, montreal.usconsulate.gov
US Embassy ✉ 490 Sussex Drive, Ottawa ☎ 613/688-5335; canada.usembassy.gov
UK Consulate ✉ 2000 McGill College Avenue, Suite 1940, Montréal ☎ 514/866-5863
British High Commission
✉ 80 Elgin Street, Ottawa
☎ 613/237-1530; www.gov.uk
Irish Embassy ✉ 130 Albert Street, Suite 1105, 11th Floor, Ottawa
☎ 613/233-6281; www.embassyofireland.ca

NEED TO KNOW ESSENTIAL FACTS

BASIC VOCABULARY	
oui/non	yes/no
s'il vous plaît	please
merci	thank you
excusez-moi	excuse me
bonjour	hello
bonsoir	good evening
au revoir	goodbye
parlez-vous anglais?	do you speak English?
je ne comprends pas	I don't understand
combien?	how much?
où est/sont…?	where is/are…?
ici/là	here/there
tournez à gauche/droite	turn left/right
tout droit	straight on
quand?	when?
aujourd'hui	today
hier	yesterday
demain	tomorrow
combien de temps?	how long?
à quelle heure?	at what time?
à quelle heure ouvrez/ fermez-vous?	what time do you open/ close?
avez-vous…?	do you have…?
une chambre simple	a single room
une chambre double	a double room
avec/sans salle de bains	with/without bathroom
le petit déjeuner	breakfast
le déjeuner	lunch
le dîner	dinner
c'est combien?	how much is this?
acceptez-vous des cartes de credit?	do you take credit cards?
j'ai besoin d'un médecin/dentiste	I need a doctor/ dentist
pouvez-vous m'aider?	can you help me?
où est l'hôpital?	where is the hospital?
où est le commissariat?	where is the police station?

NUMBERS	
un	1
deux	2
trois	3
quatre	4
cinq	5
six	6
sept	7
huit	8
neuf	9
dix	10
onze	11
douze	12
treize	13
quatorze	14
quinze	15
seize	16
dix-sept	17
dix-huit	18
dix-neuf	19
vingt	20
vingt-et-un	21
trente	30
quarante	40
cinquante	50
soixante	60
soixante-dix	70
quatre-vingts	80
quatre-vingt-dix	90
cent	100
mille	1,000

Timeline

EARLY DAYS

In 1535 French explorer Jacques Cartier became the first European to set foot in the native village of Hochelaga, site of modern-day Montréal. He named the hill above the village Mont-Royal—this was translated to Mont-Real by Italian writer G. B. Ramuso in 1556.

BANK RAID

Montréal was the staging ground of the only Confederate raid on New England during the Civil War in the United States. On October 19, 1864, 20 cavalrymen swooped down on St. Albans, Vermont. The raiders robbed three banks and made off with more than $200,000 before the stunned Vermonters could react. The raiders were arrested in Montréal.

1642 Paul de Chomedey, a French soldier, establishes Ville-Marie on the island of Montréal. He is helped by Jeanne Mance.

1663 King Louis XIV of France gives land rights on Île de Mont-Real to the Sulpicians, a proselytising religious order.

1682 Ville-Marie becomes HQ of the Compagnie du Nordouest, fur-trading rivals of the Hudson's Bay Company.

1701 The French sign a treaty with the native Iroquois, ending more than 50 years of conflict following the Iroquois massacre of the Hurons, allies of the French, in 1649.

1710 The name Ville-Marie is dropped.

1754–63 The French and Indian War breaks out between England and France. In 1759 General James Wolfe is mortally wounded during the capture of French Québec and in 1760 the British take Montréal. The 1763 Treaty of Paris cedes Canada to Britain.

1775 American revolutionary troops occupy Montréal in an effort to enlist French Canadians to their cause.

1832 Montréal is North America's second-largest city.

1844 Montréal becomes the capital of the new United Province of Canada.

1867 The Dominion of Canada is formed: Québec, Ontario, New Brunswick, Nova Scotia.

1870s Parc du Mont-Royal is laid out by Frederick Law Olmsted.

1940 Colorful mayor Camillien Houde is interned after urging Canadians not to register for wartime conscription.

1959 The Saint Lawrence Seaway opens.

1969 Canada's federal government accepts both French and English as official languages.

1970 Nationalist terrorists kidnap a provincial cabinet minister and a British diplomat, triggering one of Canada's worst political crises. The Québec government makes French the province's only official language.

1995 50 percent of Québécois vote to remain part of Canada, but in Montréal almost 70 percent vote against independence.

2002 All 24 municipalities on the Island of Montréal merge into one super city. .

2009 Montréal creates a 1km sq block—the Quartier des Spectacles—devoted entirely to culture, entertainment and festivals (✚ E10).

2014 Separatist Parti Québécois is heavily defeated in Québec's general election after only one term in office.

A view of early Montréal and fortifications (far left); a portrait of Major General James Wolfe (middle left); a picture depicts the death of General Wolfe (middle right); Montréal in winter, an ice jam (right)

Index

INDEX

Montréal 25 Best

WRITTEN AND UPDATED BY Tim Jepson
SERIES EDITOR Clare Ashton
COVER DESIGN Chie Ushio, Yuko Inagaki
DESIGN WORK Tracey Freestone, Nick Johnston
IMAGE RETOUCHING AND REPRO Ian Little

Published in the United Kingdom by AA Publishing

ISBN 978-0-8041-4347-9

EIGHTH EDITION

All details in this book are based on information supplied to us at press time. Always confirm information when it matters, especially if you're making a detour to visit a specific place. Fodor's expressly disclaims any liability, loss, or risk, personal or otherwise, that is incurred as a consequence of the use of any of the contents of this book.

SPECIAL SALES
This book is available for special discounts for bulk purchases for sales promotions or premiums. For more information, email specialmarkets@randomhouse.com.

Color separation by AA Digital Department
Printed and bound by Leo Paper Products, China

10 9 8 7 6 5 4 3 2 1

A05141
Maps in this title produced from mapping © MAIRDUMONT / Falk Verlag 2013
Data from openstreetmap.org © Open Street Map contributors
Transport map © Communicarta Ltd, UK

The Automobile Association would like to thank the following photographers, companies and picture libraries for their assistance in the preparation of this book.

Abbreviations for the picture credits are as follows – (t) top; (b) bottom; (c) center; (l) left; (r) right; (AA) AA World Travel Library.

1 Courtesy of Tourisme Montréal, Stephan Poulin; 2/3t Courtesy of Tourisme Montréal; 4/5t Courtesy of Tourisme Montréal; 4tl AA/C Coe; 5b AA/J F Pin; 6/7t Courtesy of Tourisme Montréal; 6cl Pierre Girard; 6c AA/J F Pin; 6cr AA/J F Pin; 6bl AA/J F Pin; 6bc AA/J F Pin; 6br Courtesy of Canadian Tourism Commission; 7cl Courtesy of Tourisme Montréal; 7c AA/J F Pin; 7cr AA/N Sumner; 7bl Courtesy of Biodome de Montréal; 7bc AA/J F Pin; 7br Courtesy of Les Ballets Jazz de Montréal; 8/9t Courtesy of Tourisme Montréal; 10/11t Courtesy of Tourisme Montréal; 10tr Courtesy of Tourisme Montréal, Stephan Poulin; 10c Courtesy of Tourisme Montréal, Stephan Poulin; 10bcr Mark Tomalty; 10br AA/M Dent; 11tl Courtesy of Tourisme Montréal, Stephan Poulin; 11cl Courtesy of Tourisme Québec, Linda Turgeon; 11bl AA/C Coe; 12/13t Courtesy of Tourisme Montréal; 12b Courtesy of Tourisme Montréal, Stephan Poulin; 13tl Courtesy of Tourisme Montréal, Stephan Poulin; 13tcl Courtesy of Casino de Montréal; 13cl AA/J F Pin; 13bcl Courtesy of Les Ballets Jazz de Montréal; 13b Courtesy of Canadian Tourism Commission; 14/15t Courtesy of Tourisme Montréal; 14tr AA/P Kenward; 14tcr Courtesy of Tourisme Montréal, Stephan Poulin; 14bcr Courtesy of Tourisme Montréal, Stephan Poulin; 14br Courtesy of Tourisme Montréal, Stephan Poulin; 15br Courtesy of Casino de Montréal; 16/17t Courtesy of Tourisme Montréal; 16t Courtesy of Tourisme Montréal, Stephan Poulin; 16c AA/J F Pin; 16b Courtesy of Canadian Tourism Commission; 17t Courtesy of Tourisme Montréal, Stephan Poulin; 17tc Pierre Rochon/ Alamy; 17bcl Courtesy of Tourisme Montréal; 17bl Lionela Rob/Alamy; 18t Courtesy of Tourisme Montréal; 18tr Courtesy of Tourisme Montréal, Stephan Poulin; 18tcr Photodisc; 18bcr Courtesy of Tourisme Montréal, Stephan Poulin; 18br AA/J F Pin; 19t Courtesy of Tourisme Montréal, Stephan Poulin; 19tc AA/J F Pin; 19c Courtesy of Tourisme Montréal; 19bc AA/J F Pin; 19b Courtesy of Parc Jean-Drapeau; 20/21 Courtesy of Tourisme Montréal, Stephan Poulin; 24t Courtesy of Canadian Tourism Commission; 24/25t AA/J F Pin; 26tl AA/M Bonnet; 26tr AA/M Bonnet; 27tl AA/J F Pin; 27tc AA/J F Pin; 27tr AA/J F Pin; 28tl AA/M Bonnet; 28tc AA/M Bonnet; 28c AA/M Bonnet; 28/29 AA/M Bonnet; 30tl AA/M Bonnet; 30/31 AA/M Bonnet; 31t AA/M Bonnet; 31c AA/M Bonnet; 32 All Canada Photos/Alamy; 33t AA/J F Pin; 33bl AA/J F Pin; 33br AA/M Bonnet; 34t AA/J F Pin; 34b AA/M Bonnet; 35t AA/J F Pin; 35bl AA/M Bonnet; 36/37t AA/J F Pin; 36bl AA/M Bonnet; 36br Bill Brooks/Alamy; 37bl AA/J F Pin; 37br AA/M Bonnet; 38t AA/J F Pin; 38bl Paul Carstairs/ Alamy; 38br David Sanger photography/Alamy; 39t AA/J F Pin; 40t Courtesy of Tourisme Montréal, Stephan Poulin; 41t AA/M Chaplow; 42t Courtesy of Tourisme Montréal, Stephan Poulin; 43t AA/C Sawyer; 44t Courtesy of Tourisme Montréal, Stephan Poulin; 45 AA/J F Pin; 48tl AA/J F Pin; 48tr AA/J F Pin; 49tl Courtesy of Canadian Centre for Architecture; 49tc Courtesy of Canadian Centre for Architecture; 49tr Courtesy of Canadian Centre for Architecture; 50tl AA/M Bonnet; 50tr AA/M Bonnet; 51tl AA/M Bonnet; 51tr AA/M Bonnet; 52l AA/M Bonnet; 52/53t AA/M Bonnet; 52/53c AA/M Bonnet; 53tl AA/M Bonnet; 53r AA/M Bonnet; 54l AA/J F Pin; 54r AA/J F Pin; 55tl AA/M Bonnet; 55tc AA/M Bonnet; 55tr AA/M Bonnet; 56tl AA/M Bonnet; 56tc AA/M Bonnet; 56tr AA/M Bonnet; 57tl AA/M Bonnet; 57tc AA/M Bonnet; 57tr AA/M Bonnet; 58/59t AA/J F Pin; 50 Courtesy of Tourisme Montréal, Stephan Poulin; 59bl AA/M Bonnet; 59br AA/M Bonnet; 60 AA/J F Pin; 61 Courtesy of Tourisme Montréal, Stephan Poulin; 62t Courtesy of Tourisme Montréal, Stephan Poulin; 63t Photodisc; 64t AA/J F Pin; 65t Photodisc; 66t Courtesy of Tourisme Québec, Linda Turgeon; 67 Courtesy of Tourisme Montréal, Stephan Poulin; 70/71 AA/M Bonnet; 71t AA/M Bonnet; 71cl AA/M Bonnet; 71cr AA/M Bonnet; 72/73 AA/M Bonnet; 73t AA/M Bonnet; 73cl AA/M Bonnet; 73cr AA/M Bonnet; 74l Megapress/Alamy; 74r AA/S McBride; 75t AA/J F Pin; 75b AA/M Bonnet; 76t AA/J F Pin; 76b AA/M Bonnet; 77t AA/J F Pin; 78t Courtesy of Tourisme Montréal, Stephan Poulin; 79t Photodisc; 80t Digitalvision; 81t Courtesy of Tourisme Québec, Linda Turgeon; 82t AA/C Sawyer; 83 Courtesy of Montréal Biodome; 86tl AA/M Bonnet; 86bl AA/M Bonnet; 86br AA/M Bonnet; 86/87tc AA/M Bonnet; 86/87bc AA/M Bonnet; 87bl AA/M Bonnet; 87r AA/J F Pin; 88l AA/M Bonnet; 88/89t AA/M Bonnet; 88/89c AA/M Bonnet; 89t AA/M Bonnet; 89c AA/M Bonnet; 90 Courtesy of Regie des installations Olympiques; 91l AA/M Bonnet; 91r AA/M Bonnet; 92t AA/J F Pin; 92b Gilles Rivest; 93 Courtesy of Montréal Botanical Garden; 94t AA/J F Pin; 94b AA/M Bonnet; 95 AA/J F Pin; 98l Megapress/Alamy; 98/99t AA/C Sawyer; 98/99b Paul-Émile Cadorette; 99t Jeff Greenberg/Alamy; 99b AA/C Sawyer; 100 NielsVK/ Alamy; 101l Courtesy of Tourisme Montréal, Stephan Poulin; 101tr Courtesy of Tourisme Montréal, Stephan Poulin; 101br cunningeye/Alamy; 102t Courtesy of Grand Prix F1 of Canada; 102bl AA/M Bonnet; 102br AA/M Bonnet; 103t AA/M Bonnet; 103cl AA/M Bonnet; 103cr AA/M Bonnet; 104t AA/J F Pin; 104b AA/M Bonnet; 105t AA/J F Pin; 105b AA/M Bonnet; 106 AA/M Bonnet; 107 AA/M Bonnet; 108/109t AA/C Sawyer; 108tcl Courtesy of Inter-Continental Montréal; 108c Courtesy of Hotel St-Paul; 108bcr Courtesy of Hotel St-Paul; 108br Courtesy of Tourisme Montréal, Stephan Poulin; 110/111t AA/C Sawyer; 112t AA/C Sawyer; 113 Courtesy of Tourisme Montréal, Stephan Poulin; 114/115t AA/J F Pin; 116/117t AA/J F Pin; 117cl AA/R Elliot; 117bl AA/R Elliot; 118/119t AA/J F Pin; 120/121t AA/J F Pin; 122t AA/J F Pin; 123 Courtesy of Tourisme Montréal, Stephan Poulin; 124/125t AA/J F Pin; 124bl AA; 124br AA; 124/125bc AA; 125br AA

Every effort has been made to trace the copyright holders, and we apologise in advance for any accidental errors. We would be happy to apply the corrections in the following edition of this publication.